The Conqueror of the East

SULTAN SELIM 1

Fatih Akçe

NEW JERSEY • LONDON • FRANKFURT • CAIRO

Published by Blue Dome Press
335 Clifton Avenue, Clifton
New Jersey 07011, USA

www.bluedomepress.com

Library of Congress Cataloging-in-Publication Data Available

ISBN: 978-1-935295-86-0

Printed by

TABLE OF CONTENTS

YAVUZ SULTAN SELIM KHAN

A baby's cries in the Shahzadah Palace in Amasya in 1470 announced the good news of the birth of Bayezid's son.

Nobody believed that this young shahzadah could be the Sultan one day, or he would cause a breaking point in the Ottoman history. However, during his eight years of sultanate, between 1512 and 1520, which covers only 1.28% of the Ottoman history, he became a person who changed history with his wondrous sovereignty. Even if it was unbeknownst to the people in Amasya that a Sultan, who can change not only the Ottoman history, but also the history of the world, came into the world, the whole world would acknowledge him after forty-two years.

He was the first Sultan who recognized the danger coming from the East. He was such a Sultan who occupied the largest area in a very short time in the Ottoman history, introduced a brand new continent to Ottoman, and put the most sacred mission on Ottoman shoulders.

An idealist or man of action, who pursued his dreams and did not leave places without founding his own system after conquering, a national leader who considered disorder to be the biggest enemy, one of the Sultans dominating the army in the most effective way, a gifted person establishing the most effective state system in the Ottoman history. Even though his enemies called him "cruel and bloodthirsty," Ottomans have a great respect and admiration towards him. His name is Selim; however, although he does not know it, everybody recognizes him as "Yavuz" and calls him "Yavuz Sultan Selim Khan."

Amasya

When he died, Sultan Selim I left a brand new vision behind. The following Sultans used only his seal for stamping because they could not fill the treasury as much as him.

HIS BIRTH AND HIS SHAHZADAH
DAYS IN AMASYA

I n 1470, Shahzadah Selim was born in Amasya where his father, Shahzadah Bayezid (Sultan Bayezid II), also served as a governor. His mother is Ayşe Gülbahar Sultan, daughter of Dulkadiroğlu Alaüddevle Bozkurt Bey. His mother is a Muslim and Turkish lady, contrary to popular belief that she is a *devşirme*.

Amasya is a small shahzadah city that enthralls people with its geography. The childhood of this little shahzadah was passed in this charming city of shahzadahs where mountains gather as if they hug each other and Yeşilırmak bisects in the middle. Amasya is a natural castle with surrounding mountains. Shahzadah Selim received a good education in the palace in Amasya from early childhood onwards like his other shahzadah brothers. Because his intelligence and talents were observed during his childhood, Bayezid II appointed special teachers for the youngest of his sons.

Amasya, "the city of madrasa" and "the city of students," offered him a great opportunity to get a good education. In this city, the shahzadah didn't have any occupation other than going hunting as well as getting a good education, and he appraised the opportunity in the best way. As a result of his education from those years, he acquired the habit of reading, and until the end of his life, his love for books, libraries, and reading never vanished. He became one of the most read Sultans of the Ottoman history. He was a bookworm and the people around him panicked if one of his books disappeared.

Since Amasya of 1480s was also a border city, the shahzadah, a governor of sanjak in Amasya, was considered the strongest candidate for the Ottoman throne. There is the reason the city was located on the border, and the successes accomplished as a result of the battles facilitated the recognition of the shahzadah. As a matter of fact, beginning from Çelebi Mehmed, Murad II and Mehmed II also were the banner principalities and ended up being Sultans. In addition to Bayezid II and his sons, the son of the Magnificent, Mustafa, would also be an administrator in this city. Amasya would lose its importance after the trouble caused by the other son of the Magnificent, Shahzadah Bayezid. All of these features and its connection with Ottoman dynasty made this city an important cultural center.

Çelebi Mehmed carried out the first administration of Amasya, which was added to Ottoman lands by Sultan Yıldırım Bayezid. At the battle, upon Yıldırım Bayezid's captivity by Timur, Çelebi Mehmed, taking part in the battle with his forces, was drawn to the city that is a natural fortress. He even used the city as a base of operations against his brothers, Isa and Suleiman. After that, the city gained importance as a strategic headquarters in the eastern border of the Ottomans until the end of the 16th century. After the victory of Chaldiran, Yavuz Sultan Selim returned to the city where he spent his childhood and stayed there during winter.

SHAHZADAH SELIM OPPOSING
THE CONQUEROR

He was about ten years old when he was summoned by his grandfather, Fatih Sultan Mehmed, to Istanbul together with his elder brothers for the circumcision ceremony. He came to Istanbul with his five brothers and one cousin. This was his first time coming to Istanbul and Topkapı Palace.

The giant city of Istanbul made Amasya seem smaller in comparison. A river and a sea passes through the cities of Amasya and Istanbul, respectively. Amasya was founded in the middle of the mountains, whereas Istanbul is located upon seven hills.

Horse-drawn carriages passing through Middle Anatolia used to carry shahzadahs from Amasya to Istanbul. He appeared in front of his grandfather along with his elder brothers. Then, they were all circumcised at the Palace.

Fatih, very happy to be with his grandchildren in Istanbul, looked after them closely. Once he asked them if they loved him or their fathers. Only Shahzadah Ahmed says that he loved his father more. Yet, Selim thought differently. He said that he loved his grandfather more than he loved his father. Fatih loved this little shahzadah who was very clever, and chatted with him many times, placing him on his lap.

His grandfather was at such a great place in the eyes of this little shahzadah. That he knew him as a child would change his life completely.

Sultan Mehmed the Conqueror

Years later during his reign, when a picture of Mehmed II the Conqueror was shown to him, he didn't like the picture and said: "It tried to portray the deceased Sultan Mehmed but could not simulate his likeness. The deceased took us on his blessed knees in our childhood. The shape of his face is in my memory. His nose was falcon-nosed; this artist could not illustrate him exactly. This is the first and last encounter of the Conqueror and Yavuz. Shahzadah falls on the road to Amasya. A year later, the Conqueror passed away on an expedition.

In those years, sending the circumcised shahzadahs to fortresses as governors was customary. However, while fortresses were given to other siblings, because Selim was the smallest, he was sent to be next to his father.

During the time Selim started to wait for the fortress to be given to him, and continued his education in Amasya, the news about the death of his grandfather came. His father ascends to the throne. When Selim who went to Istanbul with his mother reaches the age of seventeen, he is sent to Trabzon, conquered by his grandfather Mehmet II the Conqueror, as the governor of a fortress.

It is accepted that the conqueror side of Mehmed II stands out in Yavuz Sultan Selim, but not in his son, Bayezid II.

The Cem Sultan incident that occurred in his father's period shackled the government both internally and externally. This incident promoted an idea in the shahzadah's mind that the state administration should be gathered in one hand and the power can never be shared with anybody or any institution.

Bayezid II, father of Shahzadah Selim

THE YOUNG SHAHZADAH
IS IN TRABZON

In 1487, Ayşe Gülbahar Hatun, Shahzadah Selim's mother, was on a horse-drawn carriage in the convoy that set out from Istanbul, and Shahzadah Selim was on one of the horses. After weeks-long travel on the tough roads of Trabzon, Shahzadah Selim would stay in this small coastal city, which he came to when he was 17 years old, for 24 years. Shahzadah Selim is the second and last shahzadah of Trabzon, following his elder brother, Shahzadah Abdullah.

The long years in Trabzon gave him great experiences for his short future reign. Trabzon taught shahzadahs things about navigation, ships, and assembling a navy, which they could attain neither in Amasya nor in Manisa. Controlling the seas was the most essential prerequisite of the domination of the lands... The shahzadah, learning about the sea expedition and what a navy needs, would benefit from these experiences in the future.

Being in Trabzon gave him a chance to see the danger of Iran closely coming from the East; he would be aware of this danger with all the details, and he would not have been informed of its severity to this extent if he had been at other fortresses.

There are two people who contributed to him in Trabzon: his mother and his accompanying teacher, Halimi Çelebi. He never left Halimi Çelebi, and when he passed away on the return journey of the Egypt expedition, he would be very sad.

In Trabzon where he was an administrator he attained a tough personality, as combative as the Black Sea, with its waves hitting the coast, and as impetuous as a person from this region. The city in which he stayed for a quarter of a century shaped his spirit. Trabzon taught him one more thing, which is the art of being able to make something in impossibilities.

In one of his letters he sent to his Sultan father, he discusses the agricultural weakness of Trabzon and complains about the unfavorable conditions by saying that the necessary grain is provided from outside—sometimes it comes by ship, and sometimes it is carried from Turkmen's side, namely from the region of Erzurum-Erzincan-Sivas. He refers to the coziness of Shahzadahs administrating the fortresses with abundant crop production and says that he does not understand why they still have various demands from the Center despite this. He writes that he fulfills his responsibility for the government with very little facilities and he wades into combats against enemies.

The last Anatolian city to become part of the Ottoman Empire is Trabzon. In those years, Trabzon suffers deeply from Georgian pirates, who are settled on Caucasus coasts and threaten the city. Young Shahzadah does not show any patience to that kind of attack after he is appointed to Trabzon and walks over to Georgians. He also includes various military activities on the border.

He gained great success in one of the big expeditions against the King of Georgia. Georgians cannot dare to descend to piracy on Trabzon anymore. Shahzadah also fought with Christian Circassians, who considered themselves to be successful soldiers, showing Circassian cities that are more successful. Shahzadah Selim's name began to be heard and his reputation among soldiers increased.

Shahzadah Selim spends his spare time with jewelry whenever he finds time from army and navy duties. This habit passes to his son, Shahzadah Suleiman.

He carefully follows the events on the Eastern frontier, especially the activities of Georgian Principality and Shah Ismail, which will create serious political-religious issues for the Ottoman Empire. He writes reports on this issue informing the center of the State. Even if many stories are told during these years that he went to Iran and played chess with Shah Ismail, looking at historical facts and logic, this explanation is not possible. According to the story, Selim and Shah Ismail used to visit each other often and play chess and war games. During one of the games of chess, Selim defeated Shah Ismail and meanwhile, supposedly, he hid his ring under a stone; he found the stone many years after when he conquered Tabriz and showed it to the public. It comes to mind that these kinds of legends may have been fabricated among the public as a proof that Shahzadah takes measures against the actions of Safavids.

Shahzadah was also in a fight with Iranian forces. While on one hand, Sultan Bayezid II appreciated the successes of his uncontrollable shahzadah, on the other hand, he was annoyed by his actions undertaken against Shah Ismail. He warns his little son about not increasing the hostility with the bordering states. However, Shahzadah Selim's whole attention is on Shah Ismail threatening Anatolia. He continuously has Shah Ismail tracked and reports the received intelligence to Istanbul. Upon these reports, when his father wants him to take measures against Safavids, he makes a military operation at around the Southern region of Trabzon and secures the territory up to Erzurum. Then he walks to Erzincan. When Shah Ismail sends a new army of 12,000 soldiers to Erzincan, Shahzadah Selim completely deploys these forces with an operation he personally participates in. He relocates people who were forced to leave from Akkoyunlu lands due to the tyranny of Shah Ismail to Trabzon.

Shah Ismail is annoyed about the actions of an Ottoman Shahzadah at a little fortress and thinks to hit Trabzon, but maybe because transportation to reach the city is difficult, he changes his mind at the last moment and goes to an expedition to Dulkadirids, located at around Maraş. He had his army's heavy artillery buried under the soil in Erzincan. Shahzadah Selim, aware of what was going on with his intelligence network, captured Shah Ismail's cannons by entering Erzincan. From now on, the great work made against Safavids by the courageous Shahzadah of a little city of Anatolia had spoken.

Shah Ismail increases his threat to Anatolia and is engaged in propaganda to provoke tumult. Shahzadah Selim understands the situation is getting worse and demands that young people who want to fight come to Trabzon by sending messengers to Anatolia and declaring that he will start an expedition against Georgians. Thousands of young fighters come to the city. The expedition succeeds considerably. The participants are pleased with the trophy they get. Shahzadah Selim distributes even the part, which is to be allocated for the treasury to these devoted soldiers. He organizes the military system in Trabzon. When the soldiers see things from Shahzadah they couldn't see from the Sultan, they connect to Shahzadah Selim even more. As a matter of fact, he finds an always-ready army right next to him, which both is very scared of him and attached to him to the death.

In 1494, Shahzadah Suleiman, who is going to be well known as the Conqueror in the future, is born. Suleiman is born at a place furthest away from the capital compared to other Sultans, and interestingly, is miles away from the capital when he dies.

Although he also has a daughter and a son in Trabzon, they will pass away when they are babies. Suleiman is going to be the only surviving Shahzadah after Shahzadah Selim.

There are also emotionally charged moments experienced by the shahzadah, who is famous for his stiffness. His mother, Ayşe Gülbahar Hatun, dies in November of 1511 in Trabzon. This makes history as the first incident in which Shahzadah cries. Ayşe Gülbahar Hatun, who cannot see that her son becomes Sultan and cannot be a Sultan's mother, is buried in Trabzon. After settling in Trabzon with her son, she cannot see her hometown, Maraş once again; she is now entrusted to this city of the Black Sea. She leaves an ancient friendship behind between Trabzon and Maraş, which still exists up to the present day. Her tomb welcomes thousands of visitors in Trabzon. Selim has a mosque done in his mother's name, called Gülbahar Hatun Mosque (Büyük İmaret-Hatuniye Mosque).

The only memory of Trabzon for Sultan Selim is not only that his mother's tomb is here. His two children who are born here, Shahzadah Salih (d. 1499) and

Kamerşah Sultan (d. 1503), also passed away in this city and are buried here.

Shahzadah Selim needed economic facilities for his goals. However, the revenues of the small town of Trabzon, stuck between mountains and the sea, are quite limited. He constantly requested money from Istanbul and sent his men to Bursa to find money.

He was keeping track of the activities of Shah Ismail in Iran when he was in Trabzon. A huge uproar occurred in Anatolia because of him; Interior and Northern Anatolia were affected terribly from this. Shahzadah, observing that his father could not eliminate the threats due to his advancing age, thinking that he could not be useful anymore, considered being the Sultan. His older brother Ahmed's name had been mentioned for the throne.

Trabzon

The military activities he organized while he was in Trabzon helped his fame spread among the janissaries. Janissaries were saying that if Shahzadah Selim became Sultan, more expeditions would be carried out and the Safavid threat putting Anatolia in a difficult condition would be ruled out thanks to him. The viziers' conviction was that Shahzadah Ahmed should have been the Sultan.

FATHER AND SON IN BATTLEFIELD

S hahzadah Selim did not administrate any other sanjak other than Trabzon when he was a shahzadah and he complained about his situation to his father in one of the letters. He talked about his anticipation of his father's favor if Sultan was not disappointed in him. In his letter he mentioned the lack of facilities at the sanjak, being in a constant battle due to being at the frontier, not having enough strength left, and his request that his father need to find a solution to his condition.

He first requested a sanjak closer to the headquarters to learn what was thought about his sultanate. Because sanjak proximity is also an advantage to ascend to the throne, this benefit generally was provided for the eldest shahzadahs. Shahzadah Ahmed did not want his brother's request to be fulfilled, and he was making an effort to have it rejected. His request was eventually rejected.

Shahzadah Selim's elder brother Shahzadah Ahmed was uncomfortable with the activities of his younger brother. The secret conflict between two brothers later became apparent. The reason that caused conflict was that Selim demanded a sanjak for his son, Suleiman. In reply to this demand from headquarters, it was reported that Sultanönü, or if another closer location was preferred due to Sultanönü's distance, the area of Giresun-Kürtün and Şiran could have been granted after transforming them into sanjaks. Shahzadah Selim rejected the offer by writing a reproachful letter to his father. He reminded him that Sultanönü is far away and, up to that point, sanjaks near their fathers were given to the shahzadahs. He said that the area of Giresun-Şiran was quite rugged, with no agricultural income, and a district in which most of its population had left to join Shah Ismail. If the reason for his father's anger was due to the many fortresses and places he conquered and his fight with Shah Ismail, he explained that he had done these not to expand the boundaries of the country, but to protect Islam and Muslims. He also conveyed the message that Şebinkarahisar, which is close to his sanjak, must be given to his son, Suleiman.

Safavids and Georgians were complaining to the Sultan about Shahzadah Selim. Bayezid II was also uneasy about this situation and he was in favor of friendship. Shahzadah Selim's relationship with his father came to a breaking point. Shahzadah Ahmed was also intervening and pressuring his father about not giving Şebinkarahisar to his nephew, Shahzadah Suleiman.

While there was already a competition between Shahzadah Selim and Shahzadah Ahmed, this incident made the situation worse. Shahzadah Selim understood that if Shahzadah Ahmed became the Sultan, there was no possibility of survival, and therefore he should become the Sultan.

Sultan Bayezid II gave the right to govern of Kefe (a city in Crimea) to Shahzadah Suleiman and Bolu to Shahzadah Murad, son of Shahzadah Ahmed. Precisely in this period, there was a big earthquake in Istanbul. This earthquake in 1509 was so destructive that it is known as "small doomsday." The Sultan could not stay in Istanbul anymore and had to go to Edirne. This earthquake put the public and the military in a pessimistic mood. There were rumors that the Sultan was too old, his sickness progressed, he could not properly rule the state, and Shahzadah Selim should have been the Sultan. Meanwhile, Shahzadah Ahmed and Selim Shahzadah Korkut took action as well.

In 1510, Shahzadah Selim went from Trabzon to Kefe to see Suleiman, and he was welcomed by Crimean Khan. Shahzadah Korkut had come to Manisa and Shahzadah Ahmed had come to Ankara.

Going to Kefe all of a sudden drew a reaction from the Ottoman Palace. Shahzadah Selim said that viziers were lax in the matters of the country, they were responsible for all the problems he had experienced, and they also directed Sultan in favor of Shahzadah Ahmed.

Thereupon viziers further sided against Shahzadah Selim and told Sultan in slander that Shahzadah Selim's goal was independence and prosperity.

Shahzadah Selim gathered supporters from Crimean Khan and Rumelian governors in Kefe. Viziers told Sultan that Shahzadah Selim had to return to his previous sanjak immediately. Then, the Sultan sent his son a message that he had to return to his previous sanjak. When Shahzadah Selim declared that he rejected this offer, Sultan Bayezid II scolded him by saying: "Are you my partner in the reign?"

In response, Shahzadah said: "Why do you ban me from holy war? Give me a sanjak at the Rumeli side at least so I can be whatever you wish and I can find solace in that." He told the advisors sent to him: "I know how important it is to gain the consent of a father; however, if the intent is that I should go back to Trabzon, I will never accept this. I have never returned after I leave a place. I am ready to be beheaded and I will never recant. Let it be whatever is needed."

Shahzadah Selim was requesting a sanjak in Rumeli, which had not previously existed. On the other hand, the threat of Shahkulu revolt in Anatolia was growing. Even though Muğla and the region of Menteşe were offered to him, Shahzadah Selim did not accept the offer by proclaiming that the Menteşe sanjak is even worse than Trabzon. He also communicated that his brother Shahzadah Ahmed's shahzadahs are rebellious and he was gathering soldiers to execute them, and that he also wanted to meet his father to explain his situation directly to the Sultan to get his blessing, and he would surrender into his hands. He sent messengers several times to his father in Edirne. Finally, he headed towards Edirne with his soldiers from Kefe in Crimea.

After passing the Danube River, news came from the Sultan. He informed that part of tax revenues from Kefe sanjak, Kili and Akkirman would be given to him; however, granting a sanjak in Rumeli was impossible due to its being against the law. Shahzadah explained in the letter he wrote to viziers that his action was described as attempting to revolt; he was going to Edirne to prevent the situation in which he had been shown to his father as a rebel. He received support from the commanders of three prominent marshal families.

Upon the movement of Shahzadah to Edirne, measures started to be taken in the city. Sultan Bayezid II took action and marched towards his son. When two Ottoman forces encountered at Çukurçayırı, the emergence a battle was a matter of time. Shahzadah Selim repeated his request for a meeting by sending a messenger to his father. However, upon viziers' insistent requests that he should not meet his son, Sultan did not accept this wish.

At a time when Anatolia was burning with uprisings, Shahzadah Selim got very angry about the rejection of his requests by the Sultan. He declared to viziers that his father should leave the throne immediately and it is very essential that he should appoint one of the three shahzadahs in replacement of him. This information was never transmitted to the Sultan. It was agreed that a sanjak in Rumelia should be granted to the Shahzadah. It was decided that Semendire near Belgrade would be given to him. Shahzadah accepted this offer. As they were compatible, Vidin and Alacahisar were added to his sanjak and he was allowed to have an expedition towards the Hungarians. The Sultan also sent a contract declaring that he would not leave his throne to any of the Shahzadahs while still alive.

Bursa

The tense environment partly subsided. However, Shahzadah Ahmed was very uncomfortable about what was going on. In a letter he sent to his father, he reminded him as the eldest brother that he appealed him to reserve his other sons' rights as well. He accused Sultan of being extremely compassionate towards his children; if he could not stop these two insubordinate shahzadahs, he claimed that he could do it by himself. When a sanjak in Rumelia was given to Shahzadah Selim, he was so furious that he proclaimed that practically all Rumelia was granted to him and he only needed two things, which were the issue of a coin and the discourse of a sermon to announce his reign. In this case, he was saying that he would stay in Bursa by putting up a rebel flag and would not let anyone pass to Rumelia. He was making plans to go to Istanbul and ascend the throne as soon as the Shahkulu Revolt ended. He was trying to convince the governors of Rumelia to take his side.

The news reached Shahzadah Selim. He announced that he would go on an expedition to Hungary by releasing news to the governors and soldiers of Rumelia. In a meeting, his men advised him not to go any further since, according to the incoming news, Grand Vizier Ali Pasha, who was trying to suppress the Shahkulu Revolt along with Shahzadah Ahmed, was defeated and died. Sultan was on his way to Istanbul and decided to waive his reign in favor of Shahzadah Ahmed.

THE BATTLE OF OTTOMANS

T hereafter, Shahzadah Selim was sure that there was a desire for his older brother to be designated Sultan. He knew that if his older brother became Sultan, he would not let him live. When he observed that the previous promise was not kept, he marched towards Edirne with his forces.

Because Edirne, which was the second capital of the Ottoman Empire, was a small city, it was not difficult to conquer it. Afterwards, he went after his father to Çorlu. The forces of father and son came face-to-face.

There was extreme tension; Shahzadah Selim did not have any intention to go to war with his father. He ordered his soldiers not to lift their swords. He sent a messenger to his father and wanted to ask him why the agreement between them was broken. At this very moment, some of the statesmen supporting Shahzadah Ahmed said that this was a malicious act showing the army of the shahzadah and it needed to be destroyed right away. Sultan Bayezid II became furious upon hearing this and ordered the army to be deployed by using military force.

The military forces of Shahzadah included the collected soldiers of Tatars and beyliks, whereas his father had very well-trained Ottoman soldiers, which were troops directly under the Sultan's command. The Sultan's army's artillery and musket fire left the Shahzadah's army in the lurch.

Tatar cavalries were disbanded. Shahzadah Selim was besieged and his life was under threat. Shahzadah took advantage of his military training, which he had received since childhood. Thanks to his horse named Karabulut, he started to run away, breaking the circle around him. Meanwhile, Hüseyin Agha was of great benefit in the rescue of the Shahzadah. He was given a government job afterwards. This was the only life-threatening event and the first and only military defeat in the life of Shahzadah Selim. Shahzadah was forced to return to Kefe.

On his return path to Kefe, Ferhad Ali Pasha, Bali Pasha, and Ahmed Pasha, his men in the ship, were talking about the work to be done and expeditions against Safavids if Shahzadah Selim became the Sultan in the future. Still, Shahzadah retreated reticently. After a while, he looked up and said: "Hey you! You keep talking about the sultanate ... Even though nobody probably fully understood what the Shahzadah wanted to tell them, Selim actually told them would become a reality.

Upon their arrival to Kefe, the Crimean Khan welcomed them and said: "O my Shahzadah, this defeat is not that important. Do not be downhearted. Viziers and commanders are not inclined to Shahzadah Ahmed because of this. If you wish, let us give soldiers to your command and help you to get the throne." Shahzadah Selim did not accept the offer and said: "We did not go there for the desire of the world and claim of the sultanate. Our elder is old and he cannot administrate the country's matters truly, and he left these responsibilities to the viziers and the commanders. The enemies of religion and state revolted everywhere. My brothers sit comfortably against Jalalis and other enemies. We asked for some soldiers to defeat Kharijites, Rafizis, etc. Besides, we were going to visit our father as well. Yet, statesmen interpreted this in a different way and they stepped in between us like a wall by saying that I took action for the sake of throne and crown. What happens is whatever is destined; however, it is not befitted for us to gather soldiers and tread on our father."

Crimea

He then returned to his tent and told the people around him that he would not be a toy in the hands of Crimean Khan, that a sultanate gained with the help of their support will not be of any use, and letting Tatar troops in to their country, which had been extended by his ancestors and his father, would not befit him. He said: "If my wish had been to gain the sultanate, I would have succeeded with the help of God and without their support. I don't need Tatar's help." Khan even offered to give his daughter to him, but he does not accept that too.

Shahzadah Selim was right about what he was saying. Shahzadah Ahmed could not have been successful in the Shahkulu Rebellion. The 1509 earthquake and the following uncertainty fanned the flames of rebellion. The purpose of the rebellion was to capture the capital of the Ottoman Empire and to exterminate the Ottoman Dynasty. The rebels came all the way up to Bursa.

The first place the rebellion started was the region where Shahzadah Korkut was the governor. Rebels looted the properties. Instead of dealing with the rebels, Shahzadah Korkut went to Manisa with the ambition of becoming the Sultan. Karagöz Pasha, Anatolian governor general, and Haydar Pasha, Karaman governor general, were both dispatched to Shahkulu consecutively, and failed. After that, Grand Vizier Ali Pasha, who was appointed to repress the uprising along with Shahzadah Ahmed, was martyred during the combat. This situation in which Shahzadah Selim was desperate against rebels lowered the reputation of Shahzadah Ahmed, especially in the eyes of janissaries.

The martyrdom of Atik Ali Pasha and the death of Shahzadah Şehinşah, who was not involved in the competition among the brothers, upset the old Sultan. He was depressed with the pressures that were made towards the abdication for Shahzadah Ahmed. He ordered Shahzadah Ahmed to his sanjak, Manisa. However, as a result of the pressures of statesmen, he was forced to invite Shahzadah to Istanbul. The statesmen favored Shahzadah Ahmed and they were not concerned that janissaries take Shahzadah Selim's side. They even were thinking that janissaries would bend to their knees when they are given some silver coins and they were explaining this with a metaphor in which dogs become calm when bones are thrown in front of them. These words went quickly to the janissaries' ears, and at various corners of Istanbul they hung banners, which said: "You don't take us seriously and bring Shahzadah Ahmed; you say that we are dogs biting bones in our mouths; however, you should know that we are not dogs, but lions; we need heads as food so we swear that we will cut off your heads." However, this was not taken very seriously.

The preparations for Shahzadah Ahmed's arrival were going at full speed. On the night that Shahzadah arrived in Üsküdar, janissaries held a meeting and decided that they would be subjected to nobody but Shahza-dah Selim. All of a sudden, 5,000 janissaries poured into the streets. They plundered the houses of statesmen pro-ponents of Shahzadah Ahmed. They sent a message to Bayezid II and they requested that Shahzadah Ahmed and his supporters should leave Istanbul. They pro-claimed that if this did not happen, they would show real mischief to the world.

Shahzadah Ahmed, learning of the situation, retreat-ed from Üsküdar. Now he understood that he would not be selected as Sultan. He aimed to control the govern-ment by force; he settled in Konya to plan capturing Anatolia and Rumelia consecutively, and started acting like a monarch. That's why Anatolia nearly turned to a battlefield. Shahzadah fell to the rebel position.

Shahzadah Selim was getting news that not only janissaries support him, but also Lords of Rumelia were on his side and there were no longer any obstacles for going to Edirne. He then wrote a letter to his father say-ing that he would obey whatever he ordered about him. Bayezid II said in his message for him: "I made my son the commander for my soldiers. I swear God that this is not a trick; I let him come here as soon as possible, then whatever he wishes will be fulfilled. He should consult with me. Here are the servants, soldiers, treasury, and ready-to-use ammunition. Now is the time he can show his efforts."

After two weeks, Sultan sent another decree and ordered that Shahzadah Selim should come to Istanbul immediately and command the soldiers to eliminate the uprising of Shahzadah Ahmed.

While Shahzadah Selim was expected to come to Istanbul, right at that time, Shahzadah Korkut, overwhelmed by the pressure of his older brother, Shahzadah Ahmed, came to the capital secretly. This caused big trouble in the government. Shahzadah Korkut saw that the ambiance in Istanbul was in favor of Shahzadah Selim. He said that he was not claiming the throne; instead, he wanted to stay in Istanbul to see his brother Selim and wished to talk to him.

SHAHZADAH SELIM IS COMING
TO ISTANBUL

Shahzadah Selim set out when he received his father's order and he met and had a talk with Shahzadah Korkut for a while before entering the city. He entered the city from Edirnekapı and was greeted with a great demonstration of joy. The next day, he went to Topkapı Palace and appeared in the presence of his father, then, after the visit with his father, he went to Yenibahçe where janissaries came to congratulate him. Besides, they sent ten soldiers that they selected to negotiate with the military. Those who went for negotiation requested from generals that since the Sultan was sick and did not have any strength to go to expedition, he needed to leave his reign to Shahzadah Selim. He said that if their requests were not fulfilled, they would kill the generals. Generals reported the situation to Bayezid II. The Sultan said that as long as he lived, he would not leave his throne to anybody. Mustafa Pasha went to the Sultan, reminded him of janissaries' threat, and said that if they refused their request, the generals would be assassinated. Moreover, if he did not leave the throne by himself, they would dethrone him.

The news that his father would leave the throne to Shahzadah Selim arrived; however, this could easily be a trick that might cost his life. For this reason, he did not get off his horse. When the drop-in meeting was held, he and statesmen appeared in front of the Sultan on horseback. Father and son expressed their longing due to not having seen each other for years. Bayezid II said that there was no peace left in the East due to Shah Ismail, and he wanted his son to have a military campaign in those regions. Shahzadah replied that he would not go against his father's order, but since soldiers would serve only when they go to the military campaign with the Sultan, if he led the soldiers as chief commander, he would not be any different from a vizier, and this could be managed only with a Sultan.

Bayezid II understood the meaning of these words and left his throne to his son. Shahzadah Selim ascended to the throne as the ninth ruler of the Ottoman Empire. To prevent any disrespect, he did not have the ceremony of enthronement while his father was still in the palace. Moreover, he did not settle in the palace before his father left. Instead, he stayed in his state tent. While his father was setting of to Dimetoka, he walked next to his car until Edirnekapı, and then he returned to Istanbul after kissing his hand and saying goodbye. Before entering the palace, when he learnt that some of the janissaries were waiting to make him pass under their weapons, which are swords, muskets, or short spears, he changed his way thinking that this was a sign of defeat. If he passed under those weapons, it would mean that he would surrender to janissaries in the early days of his reign. However, Sultan Selim was not that kind of person who would shape the state administration according to the sensitivities of soldiers.

Janissaries were in the mindset of showing everybody that they are the power determining the Sultan and wanted to show this puissance to the Sultan. Some of them had intentions to control him who got the throne with their help according to their wishes. On the other hand, the new Sultan had a nature not to share his throne with anybody. However, it was not quite possible to put some extreme distance between him and janissaries at a time when other Shahzadahs were waiting to cause provocations. First of all, he had enthroning tips distributed and then declared that he would raise their trimonthly salaries. He was aware that he had to manage janissaries until there was peace and order in Anatolia.

In the meantime, the former Sultan Bayezid II, sometime after he set off, passed away on Thursday, June 10, 1512, in Abalar village near to Havza.

Establishment of the Failed Order in Anatolia

During the first years of his sultanate, the uprising of Shahzadah Ahmed was the main incident that was making him think deeply. His elder brother had settled in Konya and was acting like a Sultan, and was trying to gather soldiers by sending messages around, conducting appointments of governor generals and governor of sanjaks for sanjaks and provinces, requesting taxes, and preparing for a battle against his brother. By sending one of his sons, Alaeddin, to Bursa, he tried to attach himself to the city. His other son, Shahzadah Murad, was influenced by Nur Ali Halife and was sent by Shah Ismail to Amasya to spread the Safavid ideas of Shah Ismail.

Not only could Shahzadah Ahmed not gather the number of soldiers he wanted to have, but also many of his soldiers changed sides, hearing that Shahzadah Selim was enthroned.

Shahzadah Ahmed wrote a letter to his brother and sent his condolences for their father's death. Furthermore, he asked for the Anatolian territory as his share of the legacy. In his reply, Sultan Selim said that acceptance of this kind of request was not possible and he added that in return to being honest and not provocative, he would not harm him. However, the reports and complaints about the activities of his elder brother in Anatolia forced the Sultan to take action. It was sure that if the threat of Shahzadah Ahmed were not removed, greater issues would be faced.

Sultan Selim Khan decided to attack Shahzadah Ahmed. He summoned his son, Shahzadah Suleiman, from Kefe to Istanbul and ordered him to substitute him in the sultanate. While he was discussing state affairs with the statesmen, he received the news that a ship was seen approaching from the Black Sea and Shahzadah Suleiman was the passenger. He was very happy. He made preparations to welcome the Shahzadah. Shahzadah Suleiman was brought to the palace after a welcoming ceremony attended by all the statesmen. In the palace, Sultan Selim hugged his son. This reunion eased the troubles they had been facing for months.

After he left his son as his substitute, he started his military campaign to Anatolia on July 29, 1512. After the start of the Sultan's military campaign, Shahzadah Ahmed began to relocate constantly. There were various rumors about where he could be found. The Sultan sent some forces to follow him. When Shahzadah Ahmed was stuck, he sent a letter to his brother.

"...you had requested the place of our father. I had also aspired to that place. By the will of God, the sultanate was granted to you. You owned the State while being the younger one. What needs to be done is that we should abstain from enmity, drawing soldiers, property loss, and casualties. Now, if I take refuge to Damascus and the East with all my children, it would befit neither my dignity nor yours. This leads to commotion. I request that you give me Karaman provided that I will stay there on the condition of being faithful to you, and so the opposition and stubbornness will be over."

Although the Sultan agreed with the beginning statements of his elder brother, he did not like his demand of Karaman at all. Karaman had been all along the castle of those opposing the Ottoman Empire. The Sultan could accept if he had another offer; however, that he insisted on his demand of Karaman was the precursor of new incidents. He sent a reply letter: "What is necessary for a Muslim is to surrender to the pleasure of God. That the world is mortal is well known. Right then there is no need to devastate the country and to lead the disorder and mischief for this short life," he said.

He informed him that if he wanted to live in one of the Muslim countries beyond the boundaries of Ottoman Empire by keeping himself away from the occupations, there would be no animosity left between them; moreover, he would not need anyone with an assigned salary. However, if he moved with those who want to plot mischief, and as a result if there will be anarchy, then what will be the will of God, he said.

Shahzadah Ahmed went over of the border and while the Sultan was in Ankara. Other shahzadahs working at sanjaks came and showed their devotion to him.

It seemed like there was no problem in sight. However, when the Sultan went from Ankara to Bursa he got the news that Shahzadah Ahmed returned and raided Amasya, and he had taken the chief of the sanjak as a prisoner. Meanwhile, the grand vizier Koca Mustafa Pasha paid the penalty for seeing and provoking Shahzadah Ahmed.

The Sultan had great ideals, and he primarily needed to provide internal peace and security of the state to realize these ideals. At the times when he went on long military campaigns, there should not have been disorder in Anatolia. He began to struggle with the shahzadahs. It was obvious that the battles for the throne— notably the one during his father's reign—were leaving the state powerless and causing the bloodshed of many. For this reason, no partnership in the reign was settled as a principle in the Ottoman Empire. This continued for centuries.

Sultan Selim was suspicious of his elder brothers and had invitation letters written as if their supporters had written them. His purpose was to see how they would react to these invitation letters. There were all positive responses in the incoming letters in which the prevailing idea was to gain the sultanate by overthrowing the Sultan instead of submitting to him. This situation did not leave Sultan Selim much choice.

The longest of the battles was with Shahzadah Ahmed. Instead of being happy, the Sultan was very sad about the execution of his elder brother. He was very much touched by the situation he had been put in, and mourned for his elder brother.

Sultan Selim I, by eliminating all his brothers and nephews who could cause provocation for the throne, had demonstrated to everyone at the beginning of his reign that he could risk everything. According to him, while there was a very big danger in the East with many religious and political supporters, the state could not have had time to spend with a struggle between siblings. He sacrificed his own brothers to prevent the sacrifice of other brothers.

This solution is the biggest matter for states governed by single monarchs. In different states, several solutions were found, up to the killing of women. As for the Ottoman Empire, the solution was bitter; however, we need to evaluate this subject in the context of that era, not in today's conditions.

MILITARY CAMPAIGN TO THE EAST

The new Sultan of the Ottoman Empire departed from Bursa after preventing the strife that could have arisen for the throne. He reached to Gallipoli via Istanbul. He stayed in the capital for a few days and appointed new administrators to the sanjaks in the areas mainly ruled by Shahzadah Ahmed's in Anatolia, ruled by mainly Shahzadah Ahmed's and other brothers' sons.

He gave the sanjak principality of Manisa to his son, Suleiman, in Kefe. He moved from the third capital of Ottoman Empire to the second one. He had always loved Edirne more than Istanbul anyway. In Edirne, he both made preparations for the military campaign and followed the developments in the West. In the meantime, there were intense reform movements in Europe. He thought that this situation was an opportunity to get rid of the danger in the East, and he spent all winter in Edirne.

The most urgent issue was of course the danger of Shah Ismail causing major events, rioting, messing up the order in Anatolia, and causing the discharge of the villages and migration movements for ten years in Anatolia. Turkmen in Karaman, Antalya, and Mersin were supporting Shah Ismail. Some people, irritated by the rigid attitudes and excessive tax demands, became supporters of Shah Ismail. The Sultan had seen this danger closely during the long period between 1501 and 1510 when he was a shahzadah. The fire of sedition caused by riots of Şahkulu and Nur Ali Halife in Anatolia required that some precautions against the religious and political threat of Safavids needed to be taken as soon as possible.

The activities of Shah Ismail are narrated in Ottoman literature in detail. According to these references, the Shah cruelly oppressed the public in his occupied areas in order to impose his beliefs, and killed the Sunnis. This situation is clearly visible in the massacres of Isfahan, Fars, Kerman, and Khorasan. This region, with a high Sunni population, faced almost a genocide for not accepting the faith of Shah Ismail.

To see the seriousness of the matter, Ibn Kamal, who lived in that period, tells that the Akkoyunlu people slaughtered only in Tabriz numbered 40,000–50,000; the city was easily under Shah Ismail's control after he entered; he massacred Akkoyunlu people without distinguishing young and old or women and children. He says that the Shah even attacked the cemeteries. Ibn Kamal also states that Shah Ismail even killed his own mother, who is the daughter of Hasan Han, because she opposed him. Feridun M. Emecen, who did the first scientific study of Yavuz Sultan Selim's biography, noticed that the information Ibn Kamal gave was interestingly repeated by Angiolello, the contemporary traveler and historian of that period, and emphasized this fact in his work.

Angiolello says: "He behaved cruelly to his opponents. So much so that he massacred most of the community from mullahs to women and children. Eventually, the people of those towns and surroundings obeyed his orders and all residents of the city wore the red helmet, which was his sign. More than 20,000 people died here. He ordered a few of the notables to be taken out of their graves and be burned; he also had his mother killed."

Coherence of these two first-hand accounts given by two historians who had lived in the same period while never encountering each other or being aware of each other is clearly an evidence of the massacres. Emecen says that Safavid historian Hasan-ı Rumlu, living close to that era, had also given information that such massacres indeed took place. An Iranian historian recorded that after the Karşı Castle was captured the civilians big, small, young and old were annihilated; the *sayyid*s (the descendants of Husayn ibn Ali) taking refuge in a mosque were slaughtered by the men of Shah Ismail on account of their justification that veterans kill the small and big civilians of the places they captures without discrimination of *sayyid* or non-*sayyid*s even though the *sayyid*s said that they were the descendants of noble Ali.

The Safavid movement, with the leadership of Shah Ismail, never allows any other sect to stay alive except for those with the same beliefs and denomination in the region they dominate, and they use violence to convert people's religious understandings to their belief systems. As a matter of fact, the Alevi groups had always kept their presence in Ottoman lands and they practiced their faith wherever they had lived. This fact corrects the erroneous information that still to this day says that Yavuz slaughtered 40,000 Alevis. For this reason, it is better to consider this issue with a diachronic dispassionateness. From this point of view, extracting grudge from the history, expecting a benefit from these discussions, and instigating hostilities in the society would have no sequel other than disrupting the peace in the society. More detailed information about the data attributed to Yavuz is presented at the end of this book.

A portrait of Shah Ismail

Shah Ismail had skillfully conducted his activities secretly and by deceiving the semi nomadic Turkmen, he began to espouse Shiite propaganda in a messianic character. The propagators calling themselves caliphs had been going to the places in Anatolia where people with similar beliefs were living and had been promising a freer and more prosperous life accompanied with various gifts. In Middle Asia, some of the Turkmen groups that used to obey religious leaders introducing themselves as gods in human bodies before becoming Muslims and that continue to believe these same customs after becoming Muslims had started to adopt these beliefs.

The Shia understanding, which is based on the hatred towards Uthman and Umar rather than their love of Ali, has profound differences with Anatolian Alevis. With such an assessment, it is not quite possible to consider the Qizilbash or Rafizi groups of Anatolia as Shiites. Their belief system was some sort of "communal Islam" formed according to Safavid Sufism.

There are some people who claim that the term "gavur" comes from "gebr" in Persian, which means Zoroastrian (fire worshipper). In the *Kamus-u Türki*, the word *gebr* is defined as "fire worshipper" (it is suspected that the term *gavur* is derived from this word and has Iranian origin). According to this, the term *gavur* comes from the Zoroastrians in the East, not from the Christians in the West.

Another practice in Iran that Ottomans did not accept is the temporary marriage contract, colloquially known as Persian marriage contract or Mut'a marriage contract. Umar ibn al-Khattab repealed this perverted tradition after the conquest of Iran. Iranians, since they didn't like Umar and wanted to do the opposite of whatever he does, kept the Mut'a marriage contract, which is absolutely forbidden in Islam, alive. In their mind, with this marriage contract, they were giving prostitution a religious nature and covering adultery, which is a major sin.

Apart from Mut'a, there was another marriage contract that caused trouble between Ottomans and Iranians, which was the real marriage contract. Although the timely and strict measures of Yavuz Sultan Selim prevented Safavids to spread on the Ottoman lands politically, the cultural influence continued. To also prevent the cultural spread of Shiite Safavid ideas on Anatolian lands, Ottomans forbid Turkish girls to marry Iranians. This prohibition recalls the rule that Muslim girls can absolutely not get married to non-Muslims. The rule was summarized as "no girls are given to Persians, and the ones breaking this rule will get the bashing" was applied more strictly in the following periods that were spent with the efforts of modernization. Moreover, this rule was put into the regulations in the 19th century. This practice continued until the Ottomans retreated from the stage of the history and the establishment of the Republic.

With the permission of Bayezid II, Shah Ismail attacked Dulkadirids in 1507 after passing through Ottoman territory. Afterwards, he killed Uzbek Khan Muhammad Shaybani and sent the Khan's head to Sultan Bayezid II to announce his victory. This action was an insult to the Ottoman Sultan. Because Sultan Selim was such a ruler who always thought about protecting the reputation of the Ottoman Empire, he would not tolerate the humiliation of his State. This incident also attracted attention for creating a rift between two states.

While taking account of economic and political issues, he was trying to do everything legitimately by asking scholars about the religious aspects of the matter and requesting fatwas from them.

Scholars released fatwas about the necessity of Sultan Selim's military campaign towards Iran. In these fatwas, it was told that the actions of Shah Ismail and his supporters had nothing to do with the religion. It was specified in these fatwas that those who don't accept the caliphate of three caliphs except Noble Ali, and what's more, those who say that they don't belong to the Sunni sect become infidels.

Because Shah Ismail did not know how the issue of who would ascend to the throne would be finalized, he was not in a hurry and he did not send an envoy to carry his greetings for Sultan Selim's accession to the throne. This went against the diplomatic traditions in those years and was a sign of hostility. During the following period, when he heard that Sultan Selim removed the threat of Shahzadah Ahmed, he did not show a sign of friendship either.

Protection of Shahzadah Ahmed's son, Shahzadah Murad, by the Shah damaged the relationship even further. Shahzadah Murad was taken under Safavid protection. Shah Ismail accepted the Ottoman Prince in the winter of 1513 and appointed him as an administrator to a region of the Fars Province. It is mentioned in a letter the governor of Malatya of Mamluks sent to the Ottoman Palace that Shahzadah Murad is appointed by Shah Ismail to attack Anatolia. According to the allegations, Shahzadah Murad tried to convince Shah Ismail that if they entered Anatolia, the people there would obey them. For this purpose, he proceeded towards Çukursaad, accompanied by 1000 men. Shah Ismail restrained the excited Shahzadah and with his new order, he commanded him to wait instead of going forward.

That the Ottoman ambassador who was sent to claim Shahzadah Murad from Shah Ismail was murdered by Safavids was not a matter that Sultan Selim could easily forgive. Also, Nur Ali Halife, who was sent to Anatolia to gather the partisans, was supported when he rebelled. This action by itself demonstrated the ill intentions of Shah Ismail regarding the Ottoman Empire during the battle of Sultan Bayezid II's sons for the throne.

Another incident similar to the Nur Ali Halife uprising is the one in which Shah sent secret letters to Turgutoğulları right after Sultan Selim's accession to the throne. In a letter addressing Turgutoğlu Musa with the date of May 23, 1512, Shah stated that he sent Karamanlı Ahmed over there and was requesting them to subject themselves to him and act together. That this letter is in the Topkapı Palace shows the success of the Ottoman administrators' sources of intelligence. Before reaching its destination, the letter was captured by the Ottoman administrators and sent to Sultan Selim to notify him.

Control of the international trade routes was obtained by Safavids, which meant the economic loss of the State. Shah Ismail's efforts to acquire firearms from Venetians and the activities in which five master gunners were sent to Europe disguised as an embassy delegation, and an alliance was formed against Ottomans, were known by Ottomans.

The Ottoman Sultan was thinking that the only solution against the Iranian threat was war. These events brought Sultan Selim to the brink of war. While the course of events was pushing Sultan Selim to organize a military campaign against Safavids, despite all his hostility, Shah Ismail did not think about going to war with Sultan Selim.

The reason for this weird situation could be explained as follows: While Sultan Selim was preparing for the battle, Shah Ismail was trying to help his ally Babür to retrieve Samarkand and Bukhara. However, he could not get a result. After some minor successes, his troops, along with the allies, suffered a heavy defeat in the battle against Uzbeks in 1512.

Following this defeat, a new threat emerged for Shah Ismail, and Uzbeks began raiding Khorasan. These attacks were extremely uncomfortable for Safavids.

Making matters worse, Shah Ismail's stepbrother Mirza Suleiman attempted a coup d'état to seize the administration of Tabriz, but this threat was soon eliminated and Suleiman was killed.

In such a complicated period, the last thing Shah Ismail desired was fighting with Ottomans. It could not be expected for him to take the risk for entering a battle with his powerful neighbor, the Ottomans, in a period where his enemies were at the door. However, he accelerated his purposeful activities to wear out the Ottomans and as it was mentioned above, he continued to provoke his supporters.

Thus, he had the intention to hit Ottomans with their internal conflicts, but he was able to guess what would happen to him if he was not successful.

Before the military campaign, the Sultan requested Shahzadah Murad by sending envoys to Safavid Palace and, moreover, he wanted Diyarbekir Province to be returned to them with the reason that it was transferred to them through inheritance. Ambassadors met Shah Ismail in Isfahan. The Sultan was aware that there were some tactics that had been used since the Byzantine era applied to the ambassador visiting Shah to distress Otto-man Empire.

It is highly possible that Sultan Selim requested Diyarbekir due to his close relationship with Akkoyunlu Murad, who resided at the Ottoman Palace. Indeed, the Sultan kept Akkoyunlu Murad in his escort and took him to the Chaldiran military campaign, so he wanted to show everyone that it was not legitimate to obtain the heritage of Akkoyunlu state.

Shah Ismail gave a negative answer to the Sultan's request and declared that because Shahzadah Murad was his guest, he could not hand over a guest who took ref-uge with him; moreover, he responded to the issue of heritage lightly by saying that it was his right through conquest to own that place.

Sultan Selim decided to take an action of operational combat against the Safavids. He held a meeting with his three viziers to discuss military campaign strategy. Even though the grand vizier Hersekzade Ahmed Pasha said he was sick and could not attend, he went to the council with difficulty as a result of being called insistently.

At this meeting, the Sultan explained in detail why battle was necessary. He especially emphasized how Shah Ismail humiliated the State. However, the Pashas at the council did not have a positive thought about a war. They said that it was early for such a military campaign due to the unsettled conflicts in Anatolia. In addition, the news about the reluctance of the cavalry soldiers about a battle was reaching them.

The time had come for the soldiers, who were usually away from the military campaigns during the period of Sultan Bayezid II. Probably, considering this, Hersekzade Ahmed Pasha recommended to follow the politics of Sultan Bayezid II.

Sultan, having seen the danger since the time of his shahzadah years, was very angry at this offer. He explained the seriousness of the matter and, with the opinions supporting him, he gave an order to start military preparations immediately.

THE EVENTS IN THE WEST AND PREPARATIONS OF A MILITARY CAMPAIGN

W hile the Ottoman Sultan was trying to take measures against the threats coming from the East, during this period, the Pope in the West was calling for a crusade against the Ottoman Empire. Despite the call for a crusade, the relationship between Hungarians and the Empire (the Holy Roman Germanic Empire) with the Ottoman Empire had improved due to the accession to the throne. Furthermore, this diplomatic revival turned into a display of goodwill from both sides. Emperor Maximilian asked for a favor to be included in the friendship between Hungarian King Vladislav and Sultan of the Ottoman Empire and congratulated Sultan Selim with his letter, dated February 2, 1513, due to his enthroning as well as proclaiming his hope to continue the friendship like it was during his father's time. The Emperor was petitioning that the peace would include them through the Hungarian king, whom he considered as his relative and brother.

While at war with one side, not to be enemies with the other side was one of the main principles of Ottoman foreign policy. While there was a threat in the East, having a good relationship with the West and avoiding an attack from that side was very essential for Sultan Selim before his upcoming military campaign. The Sultan was pleased about the developments in Europe.

In his letter to Hungarian King Vladislav, dated January 8, 1514, the Sultan expressed his satisfaction due to the visit of Embassy Committee with Barnabas Belay as the chairman to maintain the peace. The Sultan was even more relieved with this diplomatic traffic. The reason was, since 1513, there was a very active frontier environment and conflicts at the borders showed a tendency to increase. The Pope's call as well was very worrying, signaling a threat coming from the West.

While the Ottoman army was on its way to Iran, a crusade coming from the West could finish everything. For this reason, the safety of the West while dealing with the East was quite important; more than any other time in the past. Now, issues seemed to have calmed down with the manifestations of friendships. Thus, Iran remained the only target for Sultan Selim.

After completing preparations, Sultan Selim moved from Edirne to Istanbul on the 20th of March, 1514. He summoned Shahzadah Suleiman from Manisa and left him again as the surrogate for the throne. He started a trade embargo against Safavids. The trade routes were under the control of Safavids; therefore, the borders were completely closed and the comings and goings of merchants was blocked. Additionally, Sultan Selim contacted their notorious enemy, Uzbeks, against Safavids.

The Sultan went to the shrine of Abu Ayyub al-Ansari to pray before the military campaign. Then he visited the tombs of his grandfather, Fatih, and his father, Bayezid II, and gave tips to the tomb keepers. These visits were going to be new traditions for the following sultans. Every Ottoman Sultan would go to the military campaign after visiting the shrines of Ayyub Sultan, Fatih, and Yavuz.

The Ottoman cemetery in Eyüp Sultan

He moved to Üsküdar and set up his pavilion. When he arrived in İzmit, a Safavid spy was caught collecting information about the Ottoman forces. He sent that spy to Iran as an ambassador and invited Shah Ismail to accept the elevated Sunnah as well as to be repentant, saying that if he did, there would be no need for a war. Otherwise, he was saying that he would act to remove this cruelty and to establish God's commandment.

He came to Konya in the June of 1514 and visited the shrines of Mawlana, Sadreddin Konevi, and other Seljuk rulers. He had the soldiers counted when he came to Sivas. He sent back some of them. Instead of a very populous army, he preferred to establish one that was easily manageable and consisted of troops who fought well. He took efforts to form his army from experienced troops and master warriors that could overcome all kinds of obstacles quickly, instead of just from regular crowds.

Meanwhile, a letter filled with threats and insults and a box containing dry opium, a headscarf, and women's clothes from Shah Ismail arrived. Shah Ismail was provoking the Ottomans like Timur did before him. By making a reference to opium, he was implying that he saw Ottoman Sultans as drug addicts who felt brave enough to fight against the Iranian forces. As for the women's clothes and the headscarf, they were sent with the meaning of a direct insult and with the implication that the Sultan was a coward.

The ambassadors who had previously been sent to Shah Ismail had been killed and Sultan Selim retaliated similarly. Now, the answer to be given for Shah Ismail's strife as well as for his insults towards Ottomans became clear; there would be bloodshed.

The Ottoman army continued to proceed. On the road from Erzincan to Tabriz, there was a shortage of supplies, and this situation caused general discontent among the soldiers and army commanders. The Safavid army was not appearing, and there were several rumors spreading among soldiers during the long walks. Sultan Selim was trying to motivate the soldiers for the battle while dealing with other business such as supplying rations. Some Pashas also participated in the complaints of the Kapıkulu soldiers and as they chose the Sultan's childhood friend, Karaman governor Hemdem Pasha, as their spokesman. The army in a sensitive state, and the Sultan's response to Hemdem Pasha approaching the Sultan and relying on his friendship was harsh. Pasha drew the most severe punishment due to his failure to consider that he could not change the Sultan's ideas. The Sultan declared his most important message clearly to the soldiers and viziers, even by risking the sacrifice of his childhood friend.

Sultan Selim, entering the Safavid border, called Shah Ismail to the battlefield immediately. The Sultan did not like uncertainty and waiting, and knew that this environment would bring several other problems. Shortly afterwards, he thought that his fears had come true.

The shoes of janissary musketeers and Azap soldiers were worn out and some of the soldiers ended up shoeless. Soldiers coming from Erzurum to Eleşgirt rebelled by saying that there was no enemy; so why do we keep traveling in this devastated country. Soldiers considered that the Shah was not confronting the Sultan to be an apology and wanted the Sultan to forgive him. According to how it was told in the references, soldiers addressed the Sultan as follows:

"O the Monarch! May the world revolve with your command! You have been feeding the army from janissaries to the others to fight off your enemy. Currently, it has been three months that you brought the army from Anatolia to these foreign lands. You had your unlimited army with an aim to capture the Qizilbash (Shah Ismail). If this Qizilbash had a little bit of courage, he would not leave his country in the hands of foreigners. There is almost no trace of them left. Otherwise, their news would absolutely come. Since the enemy is regretful and begs for mercy, could our Sultan who is the shelter of the fate show generosity?"

The Sultan said: "We are not where we want to get yet at this time. It is not possible to go back without confronting the enemy. Even thinking about it is a bad thing. But the weird thing is that while Shah's men are perishing for the sake of their master, some of the half-hearted among us are trying to make us coming all the way up here to chasten people deviated from religion to get back and nullify our efforts. Yet, we will never retreat from our way and will go wherever we are needed to go with those obeying the authority. Those who have frail-ties in their hearts, miss their offspring and families and claim such excuses say that we cannot go any further. It's up to them; if they go back, they will deviate from the path of religion. If their excuse is that the enemy is not in sight, the enemy is here. If you are real man, act with me and continue your way, if not, I can go by myself."

These words soothed the soldiers.

Hasan Can's son, Hodja Sadeddin Effendi, narrated that Sultan Selim, by showing holes in his pavilion, told Hasan Can, one of his closest men, that these holes were made by the bullets coming from the janissaries' guns who wanted to go back, and they responded to their action by hanging the shoes of the janissaries at the tip of their spears, declaring that they did not want to return. This first military campaign the Sultan undertook with the Ottoman military would be quite painful; however, he would learn his lesson and manage to take the sol-diers under his control completely.

When the Sultan told his army that Shah Ismail was coming towards them, the signs of the rebellion van-ished completely. As a matter of fact, the intelligence coming from Şahsuvaroğlu Ali Bey sent by the Sultan to gather information about the Safavid army was enough to change agenda at once.

Sheikh Ahmed, who was the man of a governor of Akkoyunlu, was spying for the Ottoman Army during this period. Ahmed said that he met Shah Ismail at Ucan and introduced himself as someone sent by Turkmen governors. He said that he fooled Shah with various words and convinced him to take action. He explained that he had told Shah that all of the governors of Rumeli and Anatolia as well as their soldiers love and respect him; thus, they were awaiting his arrival. Sheikh Ahmed had told Shah Ismail that as soon as he appeared in front of the army, Ottoman soldiers would run to his service immediately; for this reason, he had to take action as soon as possible.

It is possible that when encountering this incentive, he might have moved with his army from Ucan, thinking that the affection towards him might be due to his disciples in Anatolia he connected with; moreover, he thought that the governors of Anatolia and Rumeli as well as their soldiers could side with him. However, the more important issue here was that, with the resolute entry of Sultan Selim Khan to Iran, the image of the Shah in the eyes of his disciples who considered him as a divine entity could be shaken, and his reputation could be damaged. Shah Ismail was unable to find another way but to settle up with Sultan Selim, who was coming towards him in order not to be a coward monarch.

Another point encouraging Iranian Shah to march towards Ottomans was that there were soldiers sharing his religious views among the cavalry soldiers, constituting the majority of the Ottoman army.

According to the information coming from Sheikh Ahmed and other news sources, he had many fans in the Ottoman army, who were just encouraging him. Even the report presented by the Venetian ambassador to his Senate reflected this case. In this report highlighted by Feridun Emecen, the ambassador was highlighting that the Ottoman Sultan had a fabulous army in which all the soldiers could fight to death; however, there were some soldiers reluctant to fight due to being in the same denomination with the Shah.

The report indicated a conviction that soldiers in the Safavid Army could fight to the death due to their loyalty to the extent of adoration for the Shah.

There were other reasons encouraging Shah Ismail to confront Sultan Selim. If a supply shortage happened at the regions on the walking route of the Ottoman army, soldiers of Sultan Selim would be affected and be worn out.

Shah virtually tried to starve the Ottoman soldiers to death by plundering the Ottomans' path, the route from Erzincan to Tabriz, by clearing the crops away and by forcing the people living in that area to migrate. He set the meadows and pastures on fire so that they could not find anything to feed the animals.

Ustajalu Muhammad Khan, fulfilling Shah's orders on behalf of the Iranian army, came to Hoy and joined Shah's army after razing the whole region. Shah Ismail easily guessed what kind of challenges Sultan Selim would face. For this reason, although he was aware that Sheikh Ahmed, originally one of Akkoyunlu governor's men, was spying on behalf of the Ottomans, because he was determined to take revenge on Sultan Selim, whether the coming news was true or not had no significance for him. In addition to that, he had started the preparations of battle when he received the first letter of the Ottoman Sultan in Isfahan; then he sent out provisions one after the other to his country's fighter forces and Turkmen Khans.

Shah Ismail had gone up to Hoy along with Sheikh Ahmed. Meanwhile, he sent him to the Ottoman quarters with a task that he had to drive the Ottoman governors to his side. The last word Shah told the Sheikh was that he would meet the Ottoman army in Chaldiran.

Perhaps it's no longer important, but some of the fake letters sent to the Shah could be striking to demonstrate the reciprocal tactics. In the fabricated letters, as if they had been sent by Turkmen governors, messages were presented to support the Shah. It is not known if Shah believed these letters, but he replied and handed them to Sheikh Ahmed. After a while the Iranian Shah marched on to the Ottoman Sultan.

After learning the motion of the Safavid leader, all uncertainty disappeared for Sultan Selim. The Sultan did not like ambiguities and preferred being in a difficult situation to uncertainty.

The army of Yavuz came all the way to Ovacık after stopping at Eleşgirt-Üçkilise Çayırı-Bezirgan Suyu-Dana Sazı, respectively. The army reached the peaks of Chaldiran in two days. Here, the operation of the leading troops of Shah Ismail's army could be seen clearly. It was time for soldiers and guns to act; a pitched battle in both sides would play all of their trump cards was about to start.

He reached the Chaldiran Peaks. While two generals of Shah Ismail whom he trusted were making preparations for a battle, he, on the other hand, went on a quail hunt to de-stress his disciples, to show off his courage by proving that he was not scared of the Ottomans, and to display that he did not care about the forces of Sultan Selim.

AT THE EVE OF THE BATTLE

When the Safavid pioneer troops were seen at Chaldiran, the army adopted a battle formation, yet the two armies had still not seen each other and there were approximately 2,500–3,000 meters between them. While the Ottoman army was marching towards Chaldiran plain, a solar eclipse occurred. This solar eclipse raised the morale of the Ottoman side and was considered as a harbinger of a victory. The night before the battle was spent in a very tense and vigilant condition due to the concern of a raid. Reaching the region after a long walk, part of the army could rest while the other part virtually could not sleep, despite being tired. There was only one reason for soldiers being so vigilant: worrying about a possible night raid. The order of the army was based on the protection of the center. The consolidated center was fortified with cannons and camels.

Sultan Selim assessed the situation with his viziers and commanders. In this meeting, a decision needed to be made for an issue. The most important issue was to decide if it was better to start the battle immediately or wait one more day to allow highly tired soldiers to rest.

The Sultan wanted to learn the opinions of the attendees at the meeting before taking this difficult decision. He asked the treasurer Piri Reis Pasha how they should act on this matter. Pasha responded that they should take immediate action because some of the soldiers loved Shah Ismail and if they waited one more night for soldiers to rest, there was a danger that Safavid spies could lure them and these soldiers may pass to the enemy's side. Even if they don't pass to the other side, they would avoid fighting effectively. This situation would adversely affect the love and enthusiasm of the other soldiers and they would end up with bad results. Piri Pasha was supporting the idea of marching onto the enemy with the exclamations of "Allah Allah" and attacking them without giving them respite.

Sultan Selim also had the same conviction as Piri Pasha. One night was already spent when the army had lodgings and the soldiers in the forces who were not on call were more rested by sleeping one night. Waiting until evening and then sleeping in the next day meant to waste another 24 hours. When they were so close to Safavids, this situation could be quite risky. The activities such as setting up tents for the Ottoman soldiers to spend the night and arranging a military camp would very much distract the attention of soldiers, and as a result of this, security measures could be ignored. Moreover, it was quite possible that in the Ottoman army there were some cavalry soldiers who had a tendency to support the other side, and Shah Ismail could contact these soldiers through his men.

The Sultan did not pay attention to some of the viziers' ideas that tired soldiers would not be able to fight and achieve success. Ignoring the ideas supporting rest, the Sultan showed off his battle experience. As an experienced marshal, knowing for sure that infantry forces equipped with firearms achieve victory, he determined the strategy of the battle very well and decided to obtain his victory as soon as possible despite the military's fatigue.

The strategy of Shah Ismail against the Ottomans was based on cornering the army of Sultan Selim in a narrow area by capturing the hills of the Chaldiran Plain. The Safavid ruler was relying on his fast-attacking Turkmen equestrian units. He was taking into account that these fast cavaliers would shake the Ottoman forces. However, the Shah's biggest mistake was not to consider that he had a military strategy genius against him.

While Safavids were thinking that they would win the result with their fast equestrians, they failed to take into consideration neither the well-trained janissary troops nor the rigorous and resistant Ottoman central power. It was never occurred to Shah Ismail that he would encounter a new battle system he had never witnessed before when the pitched battle at Chaldiran started.

While his agents, who were located in many parts of Anatolia, were spying on the Ottoman army, they could not gather enough information on Sultan Selim Han's battle plans. They could not bring new intelligence except that Ottomans would use cannons.

It was not possible for Shah Ismail to know that the new system Sultan Selim used in Chaldiran would begin a new era in the history of the world wars. The Ottomans using cannons in wars would succeed not only with cannons, but also with another method used partially by Fatih Sultan Mehmed in the Battle of Otlukbeli. This tactic was based on having the central powers equipped with light firearms, reinforced by carts that could easily maneuver in whatever direction they desired.

Although some of the viziers stated that soldiers needed to rest, Sultan Selim used his experience and preferred to enter the battle immediately, ignoring the fatigue of the military by determining that infantry forces equipped with firearms would win the victory and that wasting time would bring different problems.

Another reason pushing Sultan Selim to act that way was that Shah Ismail had arrived at the Chaldiran Plain before them. In this regard, Iran had the strategic dominance.

Many historians emphasize that Shah Ismail's arrival to Chaldiran to confront the army of Sultan Selim was wrong. It has been pointed out that the Shah needed to meet Ottomans at the mountainous positions of Hoy rather than meeting here on the battlefield with a technically and physically strong army.

The main reason the Iranian Shah was going down to the plains bravely to meet the Ottoman army with great force was that he assumed that he had many supporters among the Ottoman soldiers. That the Safavid ruler knew that the Ottoman army would get tired after a long walk also played a large role in his coming to Chaldiran. Shah was convinced that the tired Ottomans would not show resistance against the Iranian army. Shah Ismail's biggest mistake was that he didn't take his rival's firearms into account. Unappreciated factors such as guns and cannons were changing the course of the war.

There were other reasons for Shah Ismail to confront the Ottomans at Chaldiran. Like playing chess, Sultan Selim constantly engaged in strategic moves and the Shah was virtually dragging his enemy to make mistakes and forcing a war. As Evliya Çelebi mentioned, Selim and Shah Ismail, when they were shahzadahs, did not play chess but, before and during the war, almost a lifelike chess would have been played.

In order to maintain a good reputation in the eyes of his people and soldiers, Shah desperately felt that waiting for the Ottomans to come like a coward did not fit the divine mission he considered for himself, so he needed to take action. Shah Ismail, predicting that his soldiers would fight against the tired Ottoman forces with great love and enthusiasm, based on his belief of their well-established faith and devotion to death, arrived at Chaldiran overconfident in his well-rested mounted troops.

Shah Ismail's men also proposed to attack the unprepared Ottoman Army as soon as they came to Chaldiran. They had such an advantage due to having arrived at Chaldiran beforehand. An attack could have been made at the moment Ottoman forces wearily came up the hills. They could also attack while Sultan Selim's was descending the hills towards the plains. Although there is no information about why Shah Ismail did not act in this way, our guess is that Shah might not have taken a risk because he had not been able to learn the Ottoman army's size.

Shah Ismail and his commanders thought about the possibility that a sudden attack against the crowded Ottoman army might not have given a desired result, but rather would end in defeat.

In addition, another reason for not committing a surprise attack might have been Shah Ismail's pride. When he was a shahzadah in Trabzon, the Safavid ruler wanted to beat a major troublesome rival heroically. His reputation would have increased when he obtained fame after a noble fight in a throat-to-throat war, instead of a surprise attack with offensive unseemly tactics, which did not suit his honor. His pride was driving the ruler slowly to the end. Another point is that Ottomans, knowing martial arts better than Iranians, were prepared for surprise attacks and raids. Strategies for such an attack were discussed way ahead of time.

Contemporary sources do not provide clear information about the size of the armies. The numbers vary from source to source. In the Ottoman sources, the number of Sultan Selim's soldiers was shown approximately as 140,000; Safavid sources magnify this number and record it as 200,000–210,000.

While there are different narratives about the size of the Safavid army, the numbers given are between 80,000 and 150,000. Only Ibn Kamal gives a logical number, and says that Iranians were about 45,000. Some of the Safavid sources, on the other hand, say that Shah Ismail had 20,000 soldiers.

The reality is that Shah Ismail's army is thought to have been composed of around 50,000 soldiers. Although the Ottoman army has been shown to be twice as large as the Iranian military power in the sources, this does not quite match historical facts. Although the Ottoman army had a slight superiority in numbers compared to Safavids, the difference is not as high as two-fold. According to the most accurate estimate, both sides met at Chaldiran with soldiers numbering between 40,000 and 60,000.

In the morning of August 23, 1514, the Ottoman army had taken the order of battle. Janissary musketeers behind the cannon carriages connected by chains at the center would hold the enemy under continuous fire. More musketeers were located on top of the cannon carriages as well. The center of the Ottoman army was virtually like an unshakable indestructible fortress on wheels with 2,000 musketeers and 500 cannon carriages.

A janissary musketeer

As a military genius, Sultan Selim hid the cannons and musketeers, forming the firepower of the army with punishment forces consisting of 18,000 soldiers whom he had lined up in front. The punishment forces in the very front were preventing the musketeers behind them to be seen. There were equestrian state troops at both sides of the main center. Because the battle was held at the Anatolian site, the right and left arms of the army were under the commands of Anatolian governor general Sinan Pasha and Rumelian governor general Hasan Pasha, respectively.

The Ottoman army was coming down to the plain with its own military layout. Shah Ismail was merely realizing the unbeatable power of the Ottomans and was trying to get an idea about the layout of the Ottoman army walking through the battlefield. Ottoman pioneer troops were descending onto the field. The punishment forces consisted of Turks, cavalry soldiers coming from Anatolia and Rumelia, janissaries, and the Sultan, along with his household troops. Shah Ismail, without moving from where he was located, was silently observing the Ottoman army descending from the hills and coming towards the battlefield.

When he saw the magnificence of the Ottoman forces, Shah summoned his commanders and he ordered them to distribute wine to the soldiers because he believed that they could not fight sober against such an army. This event was explained in the *Lütfi Paşa Tarihi* (the History of Lütfi Pasha) as follows: "Did you see how the Sultan of Rum, Sultan Selim came and stood in front of us with such loftiness and with so many soldiers. It is very difficult for a reasonable person to resist them sober. Anyone who is subjected to me and loves me should drink wine so that the job will be successfully done."

The Safavid ruler thought that soldiers would fight better when they would lose themselves. Soldiers would not even feel when they got hurt. His other strategy was to bring the families to the war. The Iranian Shah thought that when their families were with the soldiers, they would fight more zealously and to the death with the motivation of protecting them, and they would not escape the battle.

While Shah Ismail was trying to make his soldiers brave by numbing them with wine, the Ottoman Sultan Selim Khan addressed his army: "It is time to make the full effort for Islam and show the patriotism of the descendants of the Prophets. Today whoever turns his face away from the enemy is not a man." Then the janissary band started to vibrate the ground by playing the war anthem.

A FIERCE BATTLE IN CHALDIRAN

T he first collisions between the two sides happened to be among pioneer troops. When the first clashes were in favor of the Ottomans, soldiers became motivated. Shah Ismail got angry about these minor defeats and quickly launched the main forces. Because the battlefield was a place to be cool-headed, his impetuousness was the first reason for the defeat of Shah Ismail. The Iranian forces made a surprise attack to the Ottoman forces on the right side and to the center of the Ottoman army. Their aim was to raid the left side of the Ottoman army with their main forces while Ottomans were dealing with the other attacks.

Many writers and historians serving in the Ottoman army, participating in the war, or known to witness the goings on personally give us precious information about the Battle of Chaldiran. According to them, the Safavid army waited for the Ottoman army to descend to the plain at dawn and kept their position until they arrived in front of them. The distance between two armies was 2,500 meters. In addition, when the two sides literally came face-to-face, Sultan Selim Khan gave his famous speech addressing his commanders and soldiers.

Immediately after Sultan's speech, the janissary band shook the ground with their great enthusiasm playing the war anthem. The cannons and guns started an intense fire regardless of the target, which shows that the Iranian forces were within the cannon range. There was a single objective for aimless shootings and that was to intimidate the enemy forces and to scare the horses. This strategy worked. The Safavid horses were spooked and their order deteriorated. On the other hand, the Ottoman horses did not mind the sounds of the cannons and guns raising hell with all their intensity. The reason for this is that Ottomans kept their horses with them during training while shooting cannons and guns, so that they could be familiar with these sounds.

During the shootings, some of the Safavid leading troops engaged in combat with the Ottoman soldiers. Shah Ismail led the cavalry of the right wing and aimed to hit the right Rumeli wing of Sultan Selim's army. He never took the Azaps seriously, who were right in the front. They were the leading unarmored soldiers on foot with simple weapons in their hands. He thought that soon after his prospective attack, they would all be scattered in front of the cavalry and frantically run backwards into the Ottoman army. He sent his rider troops towards the Ottomans' right wing, where the Anatolian head governor Sinan Pasha was situated. By doing this, he took into account that while occupying the center of the Ottoman army with fake attacks, he would have left the center in the lurch and he would have moved towards the back of the army with side attacks.

Sultan Selim, governing the Ottoman army, immediately launched the defense tactic against Shah Ismail's sudden two-way attack. He tried to pull the attacking Safavid troops to the center as much as possible where the cannons and guns were located.

The left and right arms of the Ottoman army were deployed away from each other. It is indicated that the distance between them was about 3,000 meters. The battle intensified at the Ottoman soldiers' arm near the beginning, and then the intensity spread towards the Rumelian soldiers' arm.

Shah Ismail sent one of his commanders, Ustajalu Muhammad Khan, to the Anatolian wing. While these troops, comprised of 15,000 soldiers attacking Sinan Pasha, were fighting, immediately after that, 20,000 soldiers attacked the Azap troops at the Rumelian wing. In the meantime, he acted as if he was attacking to the center, but suddenly he changed his direction towards the Rumelian arm. It is understood from here that the attack to the center was for show only, made to conceal the main attack to be made on the Rumelian soldiers.

The fact that the troops, commanded directly by Shah Ismail, made attacks to the center as if it were their real target, but then changed direction and moved towards the Azap soldiers with a sudden maneuver, caused bewilderment among the Ottoman soldiers. In the face of this unexpected raid, they neither could get organized, nor could they keep their arrows raining on the cavalry. Before they could throw arrows, Safavid riders came at them quickly and crushed them under their horses' feet. There were many martyrs among the Azap soldiers.

Rumelian head governor Hasan Pasha put two men he trusted, Sofia sanjak governor Malkoçoğlu Ali Bey and his brother Silistre sanjak governor Tur Ali Bey, at the front to confront this attack. These two heroic brothers were martyred in this battle.

However much this bloody battle made both sides suffer from severe losses, Ottoman troops increasingly began to retreat. The governors of sanjaks from different provinces of Rumelia also engaged in the struggle, but the trend did not change much. People were martyred one by one. Rumelian head governor Hasan Pasha showed resistance against the Safavid attacks until the end. By turning his face to Shah Ismail, he even rode his horse towards him. Exactly at this time, he was wounded by a spear blow entering through his chest and exiting from his shoulder. This was the most severe of his wounds and he had seventeen more wounds. He was taken from the battlefield immediately by his men and taken to the Sultan's Pavilion, where he passed away.

The Rumelian arm was simply without a head. When fourteen commanders of this arm, including the general commander, the head governor Hasan Pasha, were all martyred, it was expected that soldiers would scatter, but on the contrary: they did not disperse, but kept battling. Their main tactic had been to create a barricade to prevent incoming aids. The battle of this arm lasted until noon.

The Safavid troops commanded by Ustajalu Muhammad Khan could not repeat the success of the other arm and could not do much against the Anatolian soldiers, commanded by Anatolian head governor Sinan Pasha. Because Sinan Pasha expected the attack to be directly towards him, there was a barricade of cannons in front of his forces, tied with chains. He also warned the gunners firmly about absolutely not shooting without his orders.

THE BRAND NEW
BATTLE TACTICS

The condition of the soldiers who fell in the battle was showing that Shah Ismail's severe attack of Shah Ismail on this side was not expected. The general expectation of Ottomans was that the main battle would have been on the side of the Anatolian branch. The battle would have been between the Anatolian forces, and Safavids and Rumelian soldiers would have supported them. While this erroneous planning led to the Rumelian side being caught unprepared and causing great casualties, it is understood that the Anatolian side was prepared. Sinan Pasha, attracting the Safavid riders attacking the Anatolian branch near where cannons were located, was successful in dispersing the Iranian forces with the help of intensive cannon and gun fire.

Shah Ismail's troops that would attack this arm were heavily shaken due to the intensive artillery fire, and the connection between the soldiers was broken completely. Afterwards, they started a chest-to-chest combat with the Ottoman cavalry soldiers meeting them. Safavids, whose troops were shaken by the artillery fire during the combat, were defeated in a very short time. Although there was a victory at this arm, still many commanders were lost. Based on what the references mentioned, Sinan Pasha personally challenged Ustajalu, one of Safavid commanders, and dropped him off his horse with his hurled spear. The soldiers around Ustajalu as he fell off his horse killed him.

The Safavid soldiers, defeated and scattered at this arm, then went to Shah Ismail and joined his troops.

The heavy fight of the two arms of the Ottoman army with Safavids lasted until the afternoon and both sides had severe casualties. So far Sultan Selim did not put the center of the army into the battle exactly and he was following the course of the struggle at the sides. The center, exhibiting a short struggle against Shah Ismail's trap attack, observed that Shah Ismail's forces were moving towards the Rumelian arm by passing through the center. News arrived at the military camp that Hasan Pasha's forces were in a difficult situation and this arm was about to collapse. Upon this news, Sultan Selim immediately ordered support to this arm. A group of janissary musketeers were instantly directed towards that area.

A janissary musketeer

The fire curtain janissaries made with their serial musket shootings surprised the Safavid riders and disbanded them. However, Shah Ismail, who did not suspect this dispatching, had already been trying to weaken the main center of Ottomans. Thus, he would have found a breach for himself to attack the main center of Ottomans.

While the attacks of the supporting janissary musketeers beat back the Safavids from the left arm, the Safavid soldiers at the center could not move around due to heavy fire. While trying to hold his soldiers started to fall apart, Shah made one last attempt from a space to the main center of the Ottomans. The Safavid troops, which could navigate with a sudden movement around the Ottoman army, could not pass from behind due to the stacked belongings of the Sultan and soldiers, army weights, and mules connected to each other. The Ottoman soldiers, realizing that Safavids were trying to walk back, dispersed Shah Ismail and his soldiers with heavy fire by returning rapidly to that side. The Shah's move resembles the situation of a chess player who checkmates himself by his own move. According to the statements of Ottoman sources, not only an enemy, but even the wind could not get in between the weights in the back. Shah paid an arm and a leg for this move. Not only did he lose his commanders and soldiers here, but he was also wounded on his arm due to the heavy fire of the janissaries. The Shah barely could have escaped from the place he had got stuck.

Iranian sources tell that other than the musketeers at the center of the Ottoman army, there were about 1,000 janissaries firing against the Safavid army from a high hill. Shah Ismail tried to gather his forces under gunfire; however, despite all of his efforts, it was not quite possible to stand in front of Sultan Selim's army with firearms keeping the battle strictly disciplined, because one of the principles of the Ottoman troops in war is discipline.

It is a rare event to create a moving line of fire from carriages by janissary musketeers in battlefields during a war. Ottomans previously used the Hungarian battalion system and after developing and adapting themselves defused their enemy with this extraordinary tactic.

Shah Ismail could barely escape from the battlefield after the Ottoman raid. After the withdrawal of the monarch, soldiers continued the battle a little longer, but they were desperate because their families were in the battlefield.

At the time of the sunset at Chaldiran, the Safavid soldiers left at the field were either dead or injured. However, most of their families were stranded in tents. Even one of Shah Ismail's wives had been caught. This woman was not Taçlu Hatun as described in many books, but Behruze Hatun. As a matter of fact, Hodja Sadeddin Effendi, one of famous Ottoman historians, tells by listening to his father that Taçlu Hatun was captured by Mesih Pasha's son during the very intensive moments of the war. She begged him to be released by offering her jewelry, and then the son of the Pasha released her by showing mercy.

Sultan Selim also gave orders after the close combat part of the battle was completed. Retreating or escaping

Safavid soldiers were not to be followed and the leftover Safavid possessions were not to be touched.

The Sultan was right about his concern on this, and he was wrecking the last plan of the Shah. The Shah thought that the Ottoman soldiers would leave their carriages to follow them, and he would succeed if they went back and attacked these soldiers. Sultan Selim was aware of this and he thought that the withdrawal of the Safavids could be a trick of war. Thus, he ordered his soldiers not to follow the ones retreating. This move destroyed the Shah's last plans.

The reason for the Sultan's order not to plunder the remaining goods was due to his concerns about the possibility of a surprise attack when the soldiers' attention was distracted. However, when the messengers spread around and brought intelligence that the Safavids were completely dissipated, the leftover Safavid goods at the battlefield were confiscated.

It is a rare event that Shah Ismail brought the families of soldiers with them in order for them to fight better. The Sultan's order was very clear about the desperate women and children left alone after the battle that they would not be touched. Then, he set them free.

The Battle of Chaldiran, representing the Ottoman battle concept very well, shows that Sultan Selim used the tactic of engaging the center, not the wing power. The duty of the wings was to attract the enemy forces to the center. The wing power was assuring that the enemy would feel victory so as to surprise them with various maneuvers by sometimes attacking and sometimes retreating. The main finishing move came from the center, standing as a mobile fortress from which the soldiers of the side arms were pulling up to the front. The center, equipped with firearms, was casting the killer blow. Many historians who did not understand this tactic of Sultan Selim at the Battle of Chaldiran use sentences such as the battle ended in a draw; however, it concluded in a clear victory of the Ottomans.

Sultan Selim is the ruler participating in the highest number of pitched battles by entering three pitched battles, which was not granted to any other Sultans. The Sultan, instead of obtaining results by using cavalry soldiers directly as his enemy did, used mounted troops as part of his tactic. In all of the three battles he fought (Chaldiran, Marj Dabiq, Ridaniya), he obtained final results by using firearms.

The Battle of Chaldiran is the first battle in the world war history in which the musketeers affected the result of the battle directly. Muskets were used at the Battle of Otlukbeli between the Ottomans and Akkoyunlu (1473) during the time of Fatih Sultan Selim; however, for the first time in the world war history, portable firearms affected the result to this degree. This tactic is a significant contribution of Yavuz Sultan Selim to military history.

According to the information the sources narrate, it is understood that both the Ottoman side and the Safavid side had casualties with numbers close to one another. Although this number changes from source to source, it is quite possible that the number of total casualties was 5,000.

In the Ottoman history, the first battle in which the casualties are at the level of sanjak chief or commander is the Chaldiran. This is by itself a clear proof that the battle played out with difficulty.

Yavuz Sultan Selim Khan did not leave his martyrs on the square; he had them collected, held a ceremony, and ordered a mass grave to be dug. All of the Ottoman martyrs were buried in the mass grave accompanied by prayers. The Sultan had a column erected with the martyrdom dates of the heroes at the head of this tomb and left them by reciting Fatiha surah many times.

AFTER THE VICTORY

T he Sultan obtained his first victory in a pitched battle after the Battle of Chaldiran and this one was like a precursor to his other victories. The success obtained in Chaldiran is a victory of military resolution, not losing discipline, and patience of the new Sultan.

The Sultan's pavilion was set at the square and he had honorariums distributed to all of the forces under his command. On the same day, he ordered an official conquest letter to be sent to his son, Shahzadah Suleiman, whom he left in Istanbul as a proxy to announce the victory.

In those years, without the blessings of today's communication, the most important communication tools were horses, and so the Shahzadah would learn of his father's victory weeks later. He also sent victory letters to Mamluks, Crimea Khan, as well as governors of Wallachia and Moldavia and provided them with information about the developments.

With this victory, Sultan Selim showed his friends and foes that he was the biggest power of Islamic world.

The Ottomans, who were usually famous for the holy wars they had undertaken in the West, took the responsibility now for hindering the possible disorders in the East. The turmoil and the uncertainty caused by Shah Ismail in Anatolia were removed in this way.

Not content with this victory, the Sultan was interested in other military campaigns to Iran; however, the circumstances would force him to go to further South.

Idris Bitlisi, the famous historian and great scholar of the Yavuz era, tells that some of the scholars, virtuous people, and artists who had to endure the tyranny of Shah Ismail with despair were rescued from the cruelty of Safavids and were released on the Sultan's orders.

After a while, the Sultan met with local governors. The Sultan sent Hacı Rustem, coming to obey him with his fifty men, to the jail and two days later he slaughtered them all. He also slaughtered Halid Bey with his 150 men, who similarly said that they came to join him during the banquet given at the council. Why the Sultan acted like this seemed strange to people who did not know him because the murder of people coming to serve him was not customary; however, the issue was later understood. In fact, this was also Shah Ismail's plan. The Shah wanted his men to infiltrate the Ottoman army by claiming to be obedient to Sultan Selim. These men hacking the army were also given a duty by the Shah to assassinate the Sultan and his viziers. The Sultan was vigilant about these kinds of cheap tricks and he overturned the plot by doing what needed to be done against these men, who were the supporters of Shah Ismail, revolting, massacring, and looting the villages and towns.

Sultan Selim came to Tabriz fifteen days after the Chaldiran Victory. He had the Sultan Hasan Mosque cleaned and performed the Friday Prayer there. The sermon was preached in his name. While there, he brought the son of Timur's grandson Bediüzzaman Mirza next to him, He took care of him attentively, and he told him that his intention was to execute the Qizilbash and then, being sad about the grieved situation of Mirza, he told him that he would return him to his throne after capturing the country of Hind and Sind. He also offered him to take him to Istanbul. With the acceptance of Mirza, Timur's grandson as well took the road to Istanbul.

The Sultan, visiting Tabriz saw the famous palace of Shah Ismail, Heşt Bihişt. The Sultan, living his life in simplicity and never liking fanfare, preferred to live in his tent outside the city instead of staying in the palace. While in this city, he met Hafız Mehmed, the son of Hasan Can, one of his closest men. The Sultan always wanted talented people to be around him and invited Hafız, of whom he was aware of his fame from when he was a shahzadah, to his pavilion, and when he heard of his exquisite voice during the Qur'an recitation, he took him to serve at the palace.

In one of his conversations with Hasan Can, one of his closest men he told him: "We have never made a military campaign to anywhere with our own desire and vision. We were assigned to act this way all the time."

Prior to the war, Shah Ismail knew the importance of cannons for the war; he even supplied cannons. Mamluks also provided cannons against the Ottomans, as we will discuss in the following chapters. However, bringing along a weapon, and using the weapon in the pitched battle in a tactical sense were totally different. Neither Safavids nor Mamluks had enough experience on how and in what way to use these kinds of weapons. They thought that cannons were suitable only for breaking down the walls at the castle siege. However, not cannons, but muskets were the ones made it hard for them to fight. These guns left the Safavid army in the lurch.

Not only did the Iranian army not have gunmen to fight against the Ottoman musketeers, they also did not have any idea how these guns would work in a military fight. As a matter of fact, according to a document, after the Battle of Chaldiran, Shah Ismail tried to start creating a gunsmith garrison. He even employed a commander of a troop of 2,000 gunmen.

There is some interesting information in the sources regarding the musket usage of Safavids. Although twenty soldiers, who served as janissaries before, made an effort to teach the Safavids how to use a musket, however none of them could really learn how to shoot a musket, some shot their faces and some shot their eyes.

Again in the same document, there is a request of using cannons and gun carriages as the Ottomans do. To do this, Iranians taking out the cannons and the gun carriages from the mud left by the Ottomans, who had passed through the Aras river and got stuck in the mud after heavy rain, made similar cannons based on these models and they could produce fifty canons together with their carriages. However, it is not clear in the document how successfully they could use this weapon.

WHERE TO SPEND THE WINTER

To determine the further strategies to follow, the Sultan held several meetings at Tabriz. He neither left a government job without completing it, nor allowed a job to remain half completed. He did not believe the success gained at Chaldiran was sufficient because Shah Ismail was still alive and could cause new troubles.

His intention was to spend the winter around Tabriz and then finish the job of Iran completely, starting in the spring. The Sultan was thinking of proceeding up to Khorasan; however, the viziers did not have the same idea. Viziers, mentioning the troubles caused by spending the winter at Tabriz, said that the most important issue would be experienced by scarcity of supplies. In their opinion, the army was very crowded; in addition to that, not only soldiers, but also load-bearing mounts and the horses, both of which had essential roles in the war, needed grasses, hay, and so on. Moreover, since Shah Ismail had burned everywhere, it did not seem possible to obtain supplies from the surrounding environment.

Viziers also tied their explanations on why they should have not stayed in this area to the existing drought, talked about the difficulties of keeping the soldiers here in these scarce opportunities, and mentioned that in the case of staying under these circumstances, opportunities would arise for Shah Ismail.

Sultan Selim had totally different things in his mind; however, although he did not like what the viziers said, he granted them their right. There was no way to spend the winter in Tabriz and it was very clear that staying here would have caused too many troubles.

The Sultan had always had alternative plans in mind. Even if it was not Tabriz, because he was thinking to spend the winter in a place close to Iran, he suggested Karabakh.

He mentioned at the meeting that Karabakh was already a place where Iranian Shahs used as winter quarters. He said that there were sufficient opportunities to feed both the soldiers and the mounts carrying the army weights. He said that it was a country abundant in food and beverages. He mentioned that since it was also possible to find supplies in case of distress, Karabakh was a good choice for the army to spend the winter.

For all of these reasons, he said that his wish was to spend the winter in Karabakh. Before making a final decision, he wanted information to be gathered about Karabakh, to see if it was suitable for the army to spend the winter. He specified that, otherwise, they would have returned to Anatolia.

None of the viziers he spoke with was a master like the Sultan. Sultan Selim, who got to know the region very well during his long shahzadah years in Trabzon, was defining his plan accordingly. Upon the news of Karabakh being a suitable place, he set off from Tabriz to Karabakh. Meanwhile, he kept his grandfather's tradition about taking the smart, knowledgeable, and wise people to Istanbul after conquests. With the objective of making the Ottoman capital not only a political, but also a science and art center, he ordered the scholars, artists, and master craftsmen to be sent to Istanbul.

Once the Sultan learned that Karabakh was available, he began to go down to Karabakh by following the Nahçivan path and passing through the places near the Georgia border.

The Sultan was taking the army through the safest way; in a sense, he guiding of the army all by himself.

The facts that Karabakh had a suitable geography, it was in a place to be able to get a supply support from the Georgians, as well as the supplies and ammunition coming from Trabzon, all affected the Sultan's decision to go to Karabakh. However, he encountered some unplanned troubles.

While crossing the Aras River, the discontent among soldiers surfaced. There was a flood, and for this reason, a considerable number of soldiers and horses were swept into the water. Becoming a martyr against a river but not against the enemy caused demoralization; to make matters worse, when the famine along the way was added to this trouble, strife began.

The angry janissaries who had losses due to the river, with the support of some of the viziers and governors, demonstrated in front of the Sultan's tent at the bank of the river, by hanging their torn clothes and piles of shoes due to excessive walking on their spears. At the same time, they also said out loud that they wanted to return to Anatolia. The Sultan's idea of spending the winter at Tabriz or Karabakh near Iran came to naught. Instead, the Sultan decided to spend the winter in Amasya, his birthplace, although he did not want to. However, even if he seemed to accept the uprising of the janissaries at this sensitive period, he never had an understanding of being guided by soldiers.

The Sultan, taking into account the sensitivity of the issue, being in the enemy's land, and the anger of the soldiers, changed his mind; however, he also took note of the people who had done these actions.

First of all, he made changes of assignment for some of the executives. He unseated some of them. Before arriving at Amasya, a difficult path was awaiting the Ottoman army. Lack of rations on one hand and heavy snow on the other hand were very much exhausting the army.

Three thousand sheep coming from the Georgian governor and rations sent by the Vizier Piri Pasha, who went to the regions of Bayburt to find provisions, were not sufficient to feed the huge army.

Due to the hardship of hunger, a couple of soldiers attacked the surrounding villages. The Sultan, always caring about the rights and the law, lost his temper when hearing of the incidents. He found the soldiers involved and executed them in front of everybody. There was no place for soldiers who performed haram activities.

Furthermore, he dismissed the grand vizier Hersekzade Ahmed Pasha and the second vizier Dukakinoğlu Ahmed Pasha for acting imprudently and failing to restrain the soldiers by breaking down their tents. To detect the unvirtuous ones among the soldiers, he banned everyone to wear white helmets, except the janissaries, doorkeepers, and infantry bodyguards. Therefore soldiers learnt their limits very well about *haram* and *halal*. The journey finished around the end of November in Amasya.

Although a letter of Shah Ismail containing messages of diversions arrived while in Amasya, the Sultan responded to him with a fairly hard message, inviting to follow the religious beliefs.

When he was thinking about new military campaigns following the winter in Amasya, he realized that his staff was not ready for this. The statesmen got used to the tranquility and comfort similar to the period of

Sultan Bayezid II. They were trying to restrain the new Sultan; however, this was not that easy.

Yavuz Sultan Selim was neither calm-natured like his father, nor he was interested in incidental issues. He had the intention of following a brave diplomacy, which was going to affect the main politics of the government. So to speak, the wagons weren't able to keep up with the speed of the locomotive engine. On the other hand, there were those placing stones on the railroads, and janissaries were at the top of the list.

It was not possible for a Sultan like Yavuz to tolerate the incidents they caused on the path of the military campaign and following that; however, he was patient. After the last incident in Amasya, the Sultan knowing very well that a ruler who cannot control his soldiers loses his power was going to show janissaries who were trying to manipulate the Sultan, who should have had the ropes in hand.

The incident started with the uprising of janissaries, not wishing to go on another military campaign to Iran. The Sultan was aware that the military was being provoked by some of the statesmen. The janissary bullies forcibly entered the houses and looted the properties of Piri Pasha, whom the Sultan appreciated very much and appointed to the vizier position, and of his teacher Halimi Çelebi, whom the Sultan showed respect to and did not allocate from himself since his shahzadah time. Piri Pasha and Halimi Çelebi barely escaped with their lives. Janissaries pretended to oppose the appointment of Piri Pasha who came from bureaucracy but not among janissaries for the vizier position.

The Sultan could not have shown patience to janissaries who held an important position in his army for being so involved in politics. Thinking the grand vizier Dukakinzade Ahmed Pasha was behind this incident, he gave him the most severe punishment. This execution did not mean that other people responsible for the matter would not be punished. The Sultan waited to return to Istanbul to punish the others.

IN FRONT OF KEMAH CASTLE

Although some people thought that the Sultan had covered the incident, the Sultan, knowing where and how to act, was aware that the military campaign path was not suitable to handle this problem.

There were two important issues that needed to be solved while in Amasya. The first one was the Kemah Castle of strategic importance and the second one was about the relationships with Dulkadiroğlu Alaüddevle.

He was trying to develop new policies for the local tribes in the East. The Sultan was preparing a foundation beforehand for another military campaign against Safavids that he would begin in the future and he did not want to leave any issues unresolved.

The news, reporting the attacks of Safavid soldiers located in the Kemah Castle on the Ottoman lands by using the strategic advantage of the castle, arrived. Safavids, clashing with the guards in Erzincan, raided the Bayındırlılar, the citizens of the former Akkoyunlu state among the people of Ottomans twice; moreover, they killed the Bayındırlı Hasan Bey and captured his family and his people.

Upon this development, an Ottoman troop immediately went to Erzincan and made a night raid against Safavids. After disarming most of them, they established Ottoman domination again.

Recent developments were showing that, for the safety of the region, it was essential to conquer the Kemah Castle. Some Ottoman governors were saying that Kemah needed to be definitely taken for the safety of Bayburt and Erzincan.

Sultan Selim thought to begin his military campaign in the spring with the conquest of Kemah Castle. He ordered the soldiers to gather. There were two big siege cannons in Tokat Castle. Thinking that he would need these cannons, he ordered them to be brought.

Two thousand Turkmen people were appointed for the recruitment and carriage of military supplies. A thousand oxen were obtained. While a military preparation of the siege was under way, the Sultan sent a vanguard to Kemah. The Safavids in Kemah immediately conveyed the message about the situation to Shah Ismail.

Sultan Selim, leaving Amasya the 19th of April, came to the front of Kemah on the 19th of May. The reason that he preferred a month-long journey was that he was following the activities of Shah Ismail during this period.

Sultan Selim was trying to figure out the connection between Shah and Dulkadiroğlu Alaüddevle. The Sultan reached Kemah through Artukova, Sivas, Merzifon, and Elmalı.

The vanguard he sent previously had already blockaded the castle. When the Sultan arrived, the intensity of the blockade was increased. The Sultan wandered around the castle on his horse. When he came back he gathered his soldiers and addressed them:

A janissary agha

"Due to the abundance of mujahedeen's sincere intentions, I want them to show careful attention to the conquest of this castle from this hour in which the whiteness of the morning shines like a kerosene lamp till the time of sunset and the first hours of the evening. It is necessary to recognize the event as a prerequisite of being a hero. First, let them throw their bravery arms to the walls of the castle as a lasso and then let the notables of the battlefield raise their bravery banners and flags."

After the speech, cannons and guns aimed at the Kemah Castle. An intensive attack started. The fire, starting from the early hours of the morning, lasted till noon. Like today's snipers, some of the janissaries climbed up a hill again and started to kill the guards one by one. This technique worked well at Chaldiran and also worked at Kemah. Six hours from the beginning of the fire, the castle was completely conquered. This success draws attention to the superiority of the Ottomans.

After the fall of the castle, the Sultan entered the castle on his horse. He ordered that the walls demolished by the Ottoman artillery be repaired. He had additional donjons added to the castle to make it stronger. He appointed one of his commanders as the commanding officer of the castle. He left 700 janissaries under his order. After staying at Kemah about eight days he continued on his way. This conquest meant that one of the arms of the Safavid in Anatolia was cut.

CONNECTION OF LOCAL KURDISH TRIBES TO THE OTTOMANS

The Sultan, aware that not all the conquests could be done with the sword, sent his one of the most trusted men, Idris Bitlisi, who was of Kurdish origin, to negotiate with the Kurdish tribes in East and Southeast Anatolia. Idris Bitlisi's meetings gave positive results and several Kurdish tribes declared their commitment to the Ottoman Sultan.

While Idris Bitlisi recounted his activities in his work, it became clear that the Sultan began these during his return from Tabriz. According to this, the famous scholar went to Urmiye first and due to the Battle of Chaldiran, he started to distribute the letters about the announcement of the victory and invitation to Kurdish governors. He obtained the first commitment from Bıradost tribe and he encouraged the Soran King to seize Erbil, which was under the control of Safavids. Later, many tribes declared their commitment to the Sultan. The commitments were so numerous so that the tribes seized Urmiye and organized attacks against Safavids up to Mosul.

Idris Bitlisi, making Kurdish tribes come to like Ottomans, went afterwards to Hasankeyf, Siirt, Bitlis, and Hizan, and held a meeting with twenty-five Kurdish governors to commit to the Sultan and fight against Safavids. The people attending this meeting were Hısnıkeyfa judge Melik Halil Eyyubi, who escaped from the hands of Shah Ismail after the Battle of Chaldiran, the Kings of Bitlis and Hizan, governors of Sason and Narman, and several other governors. These leaders promised that they would be faithful to the government of Sultan Selim and they would provide whatever help was needed. They said that since there was equality in their positions, the superiority of one over another person was not in question. Sultan Selim's intention was to make Kurdish governors select a head governor among themselves. However, the answer given in response to the Sultan's request is noteworthy. As the only way out, they requested an Ottoman governor appointed as their administrator who could gather all the regional Kurdish tribes and could lead them. They described this request in a letter sent via Idris Bitlisi as follows:

"We wholeheartedly swore allegiance to the Sultan of Islam and drifted away from the Qizilbash whose irreligious thoughts were so obvious. We removed the heresy and unacceptable innovations spread by the Qizilbash and we instated the Sunni and Shafi'i schools of thought. We were honored by the reputation of the Sultan of Islam and we started to recite the names of the four caliphs in our sermons. We strive for jihad and longed for the Sultan of Islam to arrive. We heard that the Sultan went to the Province of Zulkadriye; whereupon, we too sent Mevlana Idris Bitlisi to your presence. Our wish is that you help these sincere and subservient of servants. Our area is close to the Qizilbash land and its neighbor; in fact, it is very disordered. For so many years, these infidels had been destroying our houses and had been at war with us. Just because we love the Sultan of Islam, we expect from your leniency to rescue these people with pure faith from the tyranny of cruel people. Without your blessings, we cannot oppose them by ourselves. The Kurds live in the style of individual tribes and tribal. We are in an alliance only if we believe in one God and be the Ummah of Muhammad. It is not possible to comply with each other in other matters. The laws of creation had been prevalent in this way. However, we are hopeful that if there is help from the Sultan, those tyrants leave Arab and Persian Iraq and Azerbaijan. For a year, Diyarbekir, which is particularly the key of the conquest of the country of Iran, and Bayındırhan (Akkoyunlu), which is the capital city of Sultans, has been under the occupation of the Qizilbash soldiers and they killed more than 50,000 people. If the Sultan's help arrives to these Muslim people, both worldly and otherworldly rewards will be obtained and all Muslims will benefit from this. The everlasting imperial order belongs to the Sultan's place."

With this, all the tribes are able to successfully send away the Safavids from the regions that once belonged to them.

Idris Bitlisi frequently reported the latest developments in the region to the Sultan and mentioned the cities the local tribes bereaved from the Safavids. Thus, the sermons started to be given in the name of Sultan Selim Khan in the region including Musul-Kerkük.

That Sultan Selim dominated many cities in the region was an important advancement, but not sufficient. To ensure full control of the East and Southeast, more was needed. The region wouldn't be connected to the Ottoman Empire in the strict sense unless Diyarbekir—virtually the center of the region—couldn't be seized.

On the way back from Chaldiran, he appointed Sultan Murad, originally from Akkoyunlu tribe to recapture Diyarbekir, the city that was the center of Akkoyunlu Turkmen. However, they couldn't overcome the ramparts of the city with the troops assigned with this mission. Sultan Murad failed to connect the city to the Ottomans.

Observing that the seizure of the Diyarbekir Castle wouldn't occur militarily, the Sultan this time sent Idris Bitlisi to Diyarbekir to retrieve the city. Bitlisi, arriving at the city, negotiated with the public, answered the questions and tried to win the hearts of the people. He indeed succeeded in this. He convinced them to enter Ottoman service.

The public obeyed the requests and recommendations of Idris Bitlisi and expelled the Safavids from the city, and they declared that they were ready to accept the Ottoman administration. The name of the Sultan Bayezid Khan was read in the mosques of Diyarbekir as well.

Shah Ismail was informed about the goings on in Diyarbekir and he could not tolerate the city, at such a key location, to enter the Ottoman administration. To recapture the city, he commissioned a commander named Karahan. On his way to Diyarbekir, some of the tribes and Safavid troops joined Karahan; they numbered about 5,000. That the tribes, declaring their obedience to Sultan Selim previously could not gather and go against Karahan, showed a discrepancy among tribes. Only the people of Diyarbekir resisted against Safavids.

The insufficient forces of Diyarbekir were not enough to stop Safavids and they reported to the Sultan that they could no longer endure the situation. The Sultan, hearing the cry of distress coming from Diyarbekir, created a unity for help and gave the command of the union to Hacı Yiğit Ahmed from Diyarbekir. Yiğit Ahmed reached the city with a small number of soldiers and successfully entered the Greek door through the siege by cover of night. To mark this victory, Ottoman flags were erected at the bastions of the castle and thus intimidation against Safavids was attempted.

Janissaries

Ahmed Bey brought the letter of Sultan Selim as well to Idris Bitlisi, who staying in the city around that time, and he also brought it to notables.

In the letter, the Sultan said that he would begin military campaign in the spring, although the heretical Shah of Iran sent a messenger to convey his regret and sadness, he did not accept that, his intention was to improve the condition of Muslims, to protect the interest of the Sunnis, and to eliminate the profanity and disrespect to sacred values; for these reasons, he would not excuse Safavids.

From place to place in Eastern Anatolia, various incidents were breaking out and all of these happened when the Sultan dealt with the issues of Kemah and Dulkadir. These incidents taught the Sultan one thing: It wouldn't be appropriate to embark on a military campaign against Iran without establishing complete control over the Eastern Anatolia. He would give all of his attention to the issue of Eastern Anatolia after settling the issue of Alaüddevle, which he considered to be the biggest trouble. He would also try to exert dominance over the cities and castles with strategic importance by taking the Kurd governor in that area into his service. This strategy would be an important step for the new military campaign he intended to perform, which would bring a definitive result. Therefore, while he was heading towards Istanbul to make preparations for the new military campaign and to gain material and spiritual power, he aimed to send Bıyıklı Mehmed Pasha to Diyarbekir, which was the most essential base, and keep control over that area.

In accordance with the order of the Sultan, Bıyıklı Mehmed Pasha merged with the unions collected from the vicinity by Idris Bitlisi. Also, Sivas governor general Shadi Pasha supported him with 5,000 soldiers. When Bıyıklı Mehmed Pasha got close to the city, Safavid commander Karahan withdrew the Diyarbekir siege and went to Mardin. The Ottoman troops entered the city. (September 1515). However, without staying longer, they followed Karahan. Karahan ran away after leaving some of his troops in Mardin. Ottoman governors hesitated about whether to lay siege on the city.

Idris Bitlisi was saying that Mardin should definitely be added to the Ottoman territory and he was insistent on this idea. He went to Mardin by taking Halil Bey and about 500 soldiers with him and sent a designated advisor to the townspeople. He declared that as long as there was obedience, the properties and lives of the people would be safe; otherwise, the safety of the properties and lives of people would be threatened because the Ottoman soldiers nearby would attack and seize the castle.

The Ottomans here tried to convey a gesture of goodwill by coming before the castle, which was also showing the feeling of respect for Mardin. Otherwise, force would be the way, not convincing. The public was convinced and greeted the Ottoman soldiers with joy (October 1515).

The Safavid soldiers in Mardin immediately fled to the castle and closed the gates so the inner fortress, vigorously defended, could not be seized. There was an unusual incident in the Ottoman army at that time, and the conflict between Bıyıklı Ahmed Pasha and Shadi Pasha who supported him with 5,000 of his soldiers surfaced. With no notice, Pasha left the region by taking six governors of sanjak and 5,000 of his soldiers. It was told him that his duty given was to escort Mehmed Pasha to Diyarbekir and he the Sultan's order did not say to pass beyond the border. Despite intensive efforts by Idris Bitlisi the two pashas did not reconcile.

Bıyıklı Mehmed Pasha as well decided to leave the front of the Mardin castle the next day. When soldiers in the city also joined him, all of the Ottomans emptied Mardin. Upon receiving this news, Safavids came back to Mardin and established their control again. After returning to Diyarbekir, Mehmed Pasha waited for Sultan Selim's prospective orders. Sultan Selim became very angry when the reports of the incidents reached Istanbul.

He unseated Shadi Pasha and other sanjak governors under his order due to their unexcused leave from Mardin. Not satisfied with this, he brought them all to Istanbul and put them in jail.

With these recent events, the Sultan closed the first period on the path to be the conqueror of the East. The Sultan was thinking that the Safavid issue was left half-finished and he would return back here; however, unforeseen events would make new targets for Sultan Selim.

THE COMBAT WITH DULKADIRIDS

The head of Dulkadirids Principality, the center of which was Maraş, was Yavuz's grandfather (his mother's father), Dulkadiroğlu Alaüddevle. His grandfather Alaüddevle could ascend the Dulkadiroğlu throne thanks to Ottomans. However, he was trying to keep up by following politics of balance among Mamluk, Ottomans, and Safavids.

The governor, who was reported to be in collaboration with Shah Ismail, did not participate in the Battle of Chaldiran despite being called, and he did not send supplies after the war, despite them being requested.

Alaüddevle had seen Ottomans and Mamluks as chickens laying golden eggs and was trying to strengthen his relationship with the Mamluks against Ottomans. He did not want to get involved in the fight between them.

The Sultan sent Rumelian head governor Eunuch Sinan Pasha to deal with Alaüddevle. When Alaüddevle heard that Ottomans were coming, he gathered his principality at Turnadağ. Although some notables of the principality declared that it was useless to fight against Yavuz Sultan Selim whom even Safavids could not deal with and it was necessary to ask for mercy, he did not listen to them.

On June 12, 1515, Sinan Pasha dispersed the cavalry soldiers of Dulkadirids again with the janissary musketeers located at the back of the carriages, and then Ottoman horsemen routed the withdrawn cavalry soldiers of Dulkadirids.

Alaüddevle, participating in the battle in person without paying attention to his age, died in the clash. The victorious Sinan Pasha was promoted to vizier.

The Sultan sent an official conquest letter to the Sultan of Mamluk Al-Ashraf Qansuh al-Ghawri to herald the victory, and this was precursor of the following wars.

Sultan Selim in Istanbul after Fifteen Months

The Sultan could return to Istanbul after fifteen months. He took a rest for twelve days until the day came for the major council of the state, at which the military campaign would be evaluated; meanwhile, he traveled around the city sometimes by ship and sometimes on a horse. He went shooting in Üsküdar and Çamlıca. He met the Janissary Agha, viziers, and judges of the army on the day of the council. He accepted the greetings for the victory.

He distributed gifts to the scholars, sheiks and the poor in the three capitals of the Ottoman Empire, Istanbul, Edirne and Bursa. He visited Eyüp Sultan first and the tombs of his grandfather Fatih Sultan Mehmed and his father Sultan Bayezid II. He prayed for them.

He went incognito watch his only son, Shahzadah Suleiman, arrive at Istanbul incognito. His son had a unique place in his life. He gave audience to his shahzadah after three days. After kissing his father's hand, the shahzadah presented him with various gifts. Teachers of the shahzadah also were accepted to the presence of the Sultan.

Now it was time to settle the issues the Sultan waited to solve in Istanbul. The janissary revolt in Amasya was the most urgent matter. He considered the order of the army as one of the most essential rules of the military campaigns he would embark upon. Either he would get the military under his authority, or the military would get him. It was time to deal with janissaries who made him the Sultan and now were asking for recompense. The Sultan always used to find the instigators instead of the ones pulling the trigger, so he put pressure on the viziers to find the perpetrators of this issue at the successive councils he held. Viziers were very depressed. He even scolded viziers heavily after gently asking kadıaskers to leave the meeting at the council. It is said in the sources that the viziers' faces exiting the council were deathly pale.

The Sultan's anger towards janissaries was very extreme. He said that if he did not find those seducing the janissaries for the rebellion, he would have abdicated. The words heard in the Ottoman history for the first time caused much perplexity among soldiers and the public.

The Sultan was distressed in those days and was shaken by the news of a death. The son of Timur, Bediüzzaman Mirza, whom he personally brought to Istanbul and showed deep respect, died. The Sultan had a ceremony organized for him similar to the funerals of the Sultans.

Can Someone Get Away with a Rebellion?

He talked to the commanders for a long time to find the leaders of the janissary rebellion. He clearly repeated that if they did not reveal the instigators of the Amasya rebellion, he would leave the throne. Again, he could not get the answer he wanted to hear. He wrathfully canceled all of the council meetings.

Janissaries gathered and decided on an answer. Then they sent an answer saying, "We all are guilty on this issue and we ask for forgiveness from our Sultan." This answer made the situation even worse. Apparently they seemed to apologize but, in a way, janissaries were challenging the Sultan by gregariously taking the blame with their statement.

The Sultan understood that janissaries were protecting the perpetrators. He increased the pressure. Seeing that this Sultan was not like other Sultans, janissaries gathered again and gave the names of the leaders of the rebellion. The leaders were Vizier İskender Pasha, judge of the army Tacizade Cafer Çelebi, and head of the *sekbans* Balyemez Osman Agha. The reason this investigation was extended was that two perpetrators of the issue were the members of the council.

The Sultan was experiencing such a shock and betrayal coming from men very close to him. He wanted to know the reason for this. First, he asked İskender Pasha why he did not tell anything while being aware of everything. The pasha could only look straight ahead. When he did not answer, he was removed for the execution of his sentence. When the head of the *sekbans* was brought to the Sultan, he also could not say anything and was delivered to the executioner. The Sultan asked the judge of the army Cafer Çelebi what would be the decree for a person who wrongfully attempted to slaughter a Muslim. Tacizade said that the punishment for this would be death. Then, the Sultan reminded him of his words about Piri Pasha. The Sultan said that he unjustly tried to have Piri Pasha slaughtered and for this purpose, he provoked the janissaries. The judge of the army accepted what he had done. He did not try to defend himself and he was also handed over to the executioner.

An engraving of the Ottoman statesmen

Here it is interesting that the Sultan removed Piri Pasha from the service of the State. Piri Pasha was not a perpetrator in the Amasya events, but a victim. However, the Sultan understood that while trying to rule the government without a grand vizier, there was a serious power struggle among the teams of both Piri Pasha and Tacizade and İskender Pashas.

In the case of conflict between Tacizade and Piri Pashas, he broke the power of both groups by murdering one side and sending the other side away. Thus, the Sultan exerted his absolute power. However, he was very upset to lose such a man like Tacizade Cafer Çelebi.

He forgave Piri Pasha after a few days. Pasha was in the council again with the rank of vizier. Being in doubt about the accounts of Shahzadah Suleiman's sanjak, he postponed his leave for a couple of days. His son's tutor and head of the financial department had to give the accounts of cost and expense ledgers to the Sultan himself.

Precisely at around those days on the 25th of August, 1515, a fire starting from a zythum vendor ravaged the whole city, which consisted of mostly wooden buildings. Despite all efforts, the fire couldn't be controlled. The Sultan suspended the Imperial Council due to the fire. All of the viziers, high state officials, and janissaries worked with full effort for the fire to be extinguished. There remained huge damage. Later on, counting and inspection of the burned goods and property was performed at the covered bazaar, and viziers themselves supervised this.

The Sultan was very upset about the fire. Thinking that every negative event happening in his country was his fault, he also connected this fire to his the execution of Tacizade Cafer Çelebi.

Seeing the problems brought upon by the position of grand vizier being vacant, he appointed Hersekoğlu Ahmed Pasha to this position. He declared that he would spend the winter in Edirne. Just then, the news he was expecting came from Uzbekistan. Uzbek Khan Ubeyd Khan had conquered a significant part of Khorasan.

After staying about two months in the capital, the Sultan took off to go to Edirne. In the meantime, he launched the preparations for the new military cam-

paign. Among the military preparations, the most striking was the expansion of the Golden Horn for a new and
strong navy.

Meanwhile, the most interesting matter was the
acceptance of the grand vizier position. While most of
the time viziers competed each other and were ambitious
to become the second man of the Ottoman Empire,
Hersekzade Ahmed Pasha, appointed by the Sultan,
acted reluctantly to accept this position saying that his
age was advanced. Pasha was convinced with difficulty.

TOWARDS THE NEW
MILITARY CAMPAIGN

When in Edirne, the Sultan followed the coming news about Magyars in the West and about Safavids and Mamluks in the East. While he was fasting during Ramadan in Edirne, the news arrived that Shahzadah Suleiman had a baby boy.

This was the Sultan's first male grandchild. The newborn Shahzadah, named Murad, raised a smile on the stiff face of the Sultan. Three days later, the good news that Ottomans entered Diyarbakır reached him. The only annoying news was that Mardin was no longer in the Ottomans' possession. Thereon, various measures were taken.

With the coming of spring, ordinances were written to all governors of sanjaks, telling them to prepare for the military campaign. A new military campaign against Safavids was being planned and all of the governors of sanjaks were ordered to gather in Kırşehir.

Just then, the news came that Shah Ismail's men entered Mardin and he himself was heading towards Baghdad. It was decided that in case the Shah could enter Diyarbakır, the governor general would protect the city and the Ottoman soldiers would attack the Safavid country from the direction of Çukursaad.

A drawing of an Ottoman janissary by a Western artist

When the final decision for a military campaign was issued, according to the principle of securing the other side depending on the way the military campaign would be organized, before the military campaign to the East, the focus was given to make an agreement with Hungarians in case of dark clouds on the horizon. Meanwhile, Shahzadah Suleiman's duty was to protect Rumelia. The Sultan departed from Edirne to embark on a military campaign.

He set up his pavilion in front of Istanbul. He sometimes stayed in his pavilion at the military camp and sometimes in the Topkapı Palace; he took care of all the details of the military campaign.

In the meantime, the clashes with the Safavids in the East were proceeding. Mamluks were also involved in this fight. There was arduous combat to rule over Mardin. In the war, the Ottomans were defeated unexpectedly against the Safavids.

Never using the words Ottomans and defeat side by side, the Sultan was furious about this news. Only viziers participated in the council meeting held on the 26th of April, 1516, which lasted from morning till night.

The Sultan's anger in no way subsided. He gave new assignments. He dragged off some of the viziers whom he thought to be delinquent to the prison. He also changed the grand vizier and gave the seal to Sinan Pasha. He forgave Piri Pasha and Hersekzade in prison upon the request the new grand vizier. The following day, Grand Vizier Sinan Pasha was sent on ahead along with a portion of the army to Diyarbakır for help. Yavuz bid farewell to the grand vizier personally. He himself took the road afterwards.

The battle escalated in Diyarbakır. Ottoman forces were shut in the Diyarbakır Castle. Anatolian governors of sanjaks came to Diyarbakır's aid, along with paid cavalrymen. Ottoman forces, receiving the support of Kurdish governors in the region, walked up to Safavids. They concluded the battle with victory. Good tidings of the victory was delivered first to the Grand Vizier Sinan Pasha, who came all the way to Kayseri, and then to Sultan Selim in Akşehir.

The seal of Yavuz Sultan Selim

Meanwhile, Mamluk envoys negotiated with Shah Ismail by going up to Hemedan. Mamluk envoys gave an assurance that they could be alliances if they fulfilled certain conditions.

The events changed the direction of the military campaign; Sultan Selim intended to pursue in the East towards the South.

SULTAN SELIM IS ON
THE WAY TO EGYPT

S ultan Selim had given all of his attention to the East, where the danger was coming from. Although the danger of Shah Ismail was prevented through the Chaldiran victory and the following activities, this situation was temporary. The Shah might have caused much bigger commotion, and for this reason measures needed to be taken.

The elimination of Dulkadirids via the Battle of Turnadağ ruined the already troubled relationship between Mamluks, who saw themselves as the protectors of this principality, and the Ottomans.

The Mamluk-Ottoman relationship was tightened because Yıldırım Bayezid extended the state lands up to Malatya, and Fatih Sultan Mehmed attempted to fix the waterways on the pilgrimage route.

In the period of Sultan Bayezid II, the patronage politics of Adana-based Ramazanoğulları and Maraş-based Dulkadirids brought two states face-to-face. At the same time, when there was a Portuguese threat on the Holy Lands of Islam, Mamluks had requested help from Ottomans and Bayezid II made soldier and weapon shipments to the region, leaving the competition aside.

Adana Ceyhan River

Sultan Selim tried to continue the friendship with the Mamluk Sultan Al-Ashraf Qansuh al-Ghawri during the first period he ascended to the throne. When he ascended to the throne, the Sultan accepted the greetings of Mamluks but he could not get any answer for his request about confronting Shah Ismail.

Although his stance against all of the elements causing sedition was known, Mamluks were still keeping sons of Shahzadah Ahmed under their auspices. It wasn't possible that Sultan would tolerate this.

On the other hand, Al-Ashraf Qansuh al-Ghawri got flustered. He started draw a meaning out of all movements of Sultan Selim. He rapidly relocated near the border and he even sent emissaries to Shah Ismail by ignoring the fact that the Ottoman Sultan declared that he would go for a military campaign against Iran, which would have caused the events change into a different course.

Sultan Selim had only one target: Iran. It was obvious that whoever dominated Egypt would be the leader of the Islamic world. From an economic perspective, controlling the trade routes was also desirable. However, the most important point for Sultan Selim to obtain Egypt was that Mamluks were incapable of protecting the Holy Land. The Holy Land was under threat by Christians worse than ever before in the history. The Portuguese threat was making the people of Mecca and Medina anxious, and this concern shared all over the Islamic world. Egyptian scholars sent a message to the Sultan asking him to dominate those areas and to terminate the Mamluk administration. There were even those who gave secret letters to Ottoman envoys visiting Egypt. This situation was forcing the Ottoman Empire to safeguard the region as a savior.

In his book, *Tajiu't-Tawarih*, Hodja Sadeddin Effendi, one of the famous historians of the Ottoman Empire, narrates an incident he heard from his father Hasan Can who served the Sultan closely:

"Hasan Can tells of one of the dreams of Chief White Eunuch Hasan Agha and he was reluctant to reveal it. Hasan Agha saw in his dream that there was a knock on the door and when he opened the door he saw many people standing in Arabic costume carrying flags and weapons, and the one knocking on the door among four people next to the door was carrying 'a white flag.' This person introduced himself as Ali and others as Abu Bakr, Uthman, and Umar, may God be pleased with them, and says that the rest were the Companions. The blessed Prophet, peace and blessing be upon him, sent them and conveyed a message to Sultan Selim Khan. The message of the Prophet was: 'Let him come here since the service of the two holy cities was decreed upon him.' After listening to the dream, Hasan Can told it to the Sultan at once. The Sultan got the answer he was expecting as well. He told Hasan Can: "Haven't we told you that we did not take action without a reason?"

Egypt was in Sultan Selim's mind now; he was not focused on Iran anymore. The duty of protection and lookout of the Holy Lands were given to him. This dream probably had been seen during the military campaign. When going for the military campaign, the idea was clearly to take precautions against the incidents in the East and eliminating the issue of Shah Ismail completely.

It is told in the sources of that period that when Diyarbakır governor general Bıyıklı Mehmed Bey declared the action of Safavid Khan Karahan against Diyarbakır and asked for a help, the Sultan immediately departed from Edirne. The political developments arisen

with the Sultan's arrival to Elbistan frontiers also affected the change of the target from Iran to Egypt.

The most apparent reason of the military campaign
is that the Mamluk Sultan Al-Ashraf Qansuh al-Ghawri
along with his army, and Shahzadah Kasım, one of sons
of Shahzadah Ahmed, came all the way to Aleppo and
contacted Shah Ismail based on intelligence from an
Ottoman spy. Al-Ghawri's men said that if Sultan Selim
eliminated Shah Ismail, it would be their turn; for this
reason, the Egyptian soldiers needed to get ready and be
dropped off at Aleppo. According to them, it was necessary to deploy the Ottoman forces in that area before the
Ottoman Sultan arrived. Al-Ghawri complied with
these words and started to travel to Damascus. The
grand vizier Sinan Pasha transmitted the news to the
Sultan immediately.

In his first biographical book called *Yavuz Sultan
Selim*, Professor Feridun Emecen proves that the military
campaign to Egypt was not planned ahead as opposed to
the information in the contemporary works about Yavuz
Sultan Selim. According to him, the writers, the witnesses of that period, never mention plans. Idrıs-i Bitlisi,
being close to the Sultan, writes that Selim I took the
road to conquer Iran.

Four months before (March 1516) the military campaign, Al-Ghawri, uncomfortable about the embargo
and trade ban at the Eastern boundary, wrote a letter in
which he addressed the Sultan as "my son majesty,"

complaining about the trade ban and expressing his concerns that the Sultan would march towards Egypt from the land and the sea to Sultan Selim saying: "*Alhamdulillah* (all praise be to God) we are the Sultans of the people of Islam; since those under our verdict are the Believers and Almohads but not Kharijites, Scholar should not give *fatwa* for their death." He declared that two Muslim states should maintain friendship between themselves.

The letter reached to the Sultan at around the time when the decision of military campaign was made, and the Sultan clearly mentioned in his reply in which he addressed Al-Ghawri as "my dad" that all of the preparations were for Shah Ismail. He also explained why he needed to go on another military campaign and he did not have any ill intention towards Mamluk lands. It was reported that the Eastern border was closed due to the Safavid threat; however, people coming from Aleppo and Alexandria who did not have any Asian property were not interfered with. However, he also reminded him that if he did not consent to this operation against the enemies of the religion and if he opposed it, at that time he would have taken refuge at the discretion of God. He also mentioned that the preparations at sea were intended for defense. At the end of his letter, the Sultan asked for prayers both from the Sultan and the people of the two Holy Cities.

The negotiations between Al-Ghawri with Shah İsmail were known to the Ottomans, and the reason of his departure from Cairo was to make an alliance with Shah Ismail and to prevent the passage of Ottoman army.

A portrait of Al-Ashraf Qansuh al-Ghawri

Al-Ghawri, along with Abbasid Caliph Al-Mutawakkil, leading commanders of the state, Shahzadah Kasım, as well as 20,000 soldiers, came to Damascus from Cairo. Hearing that Sultan Selim started to move from Istanbul, he arrived at Aleppo, which was close to the Ottoman borders. Meanwhile, the Ottoman forces were on their way from Konya to Kayseri.

This situation forced Yavuz Sultan Selim to change all of his plans. By going to the border, Al-Ghawri drew the attention of the Ottomans to himself; if asked, he would say that he pursued a goal to get a precaution as soon as possible against the Ottoman assault and to dissuade the Ottoman Sultan.

On the other hand, Shah Ismail mobilized his army to join Mamluks; however, since the gateways were under the control of the Ottomans, he could not proceed.

THE SULTAN IS GOING ON A NEW MILITARY CAMPAIGN

Sultan Selim departed on the military campaign five weeks after the grand vizier Sinan Pasha. He appointed Piri Mehmed Pasha and Hersekzade Ahmed Pasha, whom he pardoned after dismissing them as guards of Istanbul and Bursa, respectively. Before meeting Sinan Pasha, the Sultan ordered Hersek Sanjak Governor Evranosoğlu and Tırhala Governor Sinan to build a bridge over the Euphrates. Although a request to build a bridge was requested to the Mamluk chief, the answer was negative and the passage of the Ottoman forces was prevented. This action damaged the Ottomans' good relationship with Mamluks. When the Ottoman Sultan was informed that the Mamluk Sultan moved to Aleppo near the Ottoman border, he didn't allow the Ottoman soldiers to pass through Mamluk land, and he sent the Malatya governor some orders, Yavuz perceived this action as a clear sign of enmity.

The Mamluk chief of Malatya had sent a *qadi* as an envoy to Sinan Pasha. The qadi told Sinan Pasha that

Al-Ashraf Qansuh al-Ghawri, the Mamluk Sultan, came to Aleppo to reconcile between Yavuz and Shah Ismail and he asked him to return Istanbul, meet the Sultan, and postpone his expedition. The envoy was unaware that the Ottoman Sultan came all the way to Elbistan. He even said that if Sinan Pasha permitted, he wanted to go to Istanbul for legation. The Grand Vizier laughingly told him: "Your intention is to go to the capital city of Istanbul, let me take you to the Sultan." The envoy was very surprised and when he found himself at the Sultan's presence, he really got in a tizzy. While trying to control his excitement, he presented Al-Ghawri's letter to the Sultan.

Yavuz Sultan Selim reading the letter turned to the envoy and said: "Someone who wants to reconcile two adversaries doesn't come with such a large number of soldiers and weapons; on the contrary, he sits on his throne and just sends an envoy with the necessary message; however, your Sultan wants to prevent me to fight against Shah Ismail. This being the case, we gave up attacking Shah Ismail and made Al-Ghawri our target."

When the *qadi* asked, "Do you have any evidence to prove the relationship between our Sultan and the Shah?", Sultan Selim became furious. He ordered the judges of the army to take away the qadi of Mamluk. The judge of the army invited some witnesses and they testified before the envoy that the envoys of the Shah went to the Sultan. Al-Ghawri was proven guilty of the offense for helping Shah Ismail. The Sultan informed the qadi that in spite of everything, he wished the peace between two sides would continue.

Sultan Selim Khan did not explain the target of the military campaign until the 30th of July, when he lodged around Tohma River after passing through Malatya Plain.

The alliance of Mamluks with Shah Ismail and the threat of Portuguese on the Holy Land were discussed in detail. Yavuz asked: "What is the decree of God Almighty in this situation?" and the people in the council answered: "The first duty of the Sultan is to remove the harmful thorns on the road, and then he would step on the track God showed." The new target was identified as Aleppo.

In the council he gathered that day, he said: "My intention is to go for a military campaign against the person called Shah Ismail. However, the Mamluk ruler comes to Aleppo with his soldiers to support that infidel." As the tribal leaders said when the Ottoman army entered the Diyarbakır region: "They are causing sedition...", all of the governors at the meeting stood up and finished the meeting by saying: "The Sultan of the Mamluk walks like a bandit; that being the case, we expect our Sultan to be our leader in front of us and we line up behind him. With our body and soul we go to the Egyptian Sultan and fight against his soldiers. With the grace and help of Almighty God, we deploy the enemy's army and spread your reputation around the world."

A man was sent to Istanbul to ask what the religious aspect was regarding changing the direction of the military campaign. A fatwa was requested from the Mufti and scholars. In reply, the military campaign was allowed.

Idris Bitlisi, one of the famous historians of the Yavuz era, says that the main target of the military campaign was to enter the Iranian land and "to exterminate the Qizilbash heretics"; however, since the Egyptian and Damascus Circassians tended to block the road to prevent the Mujahedeen Ottoman army, it was decided to walk towards the southern side for the purpose of eliminating a group of mischief-makers.

The unacceptable requests of Al-Ghawri in his late attempt of sending an envoy did not improve the relations; on the contrary, it made everything worse and destroyed all hopes for peace.

In the 5th of August, 1516, the Sultan departed from Malatya plain and changed the direction of the army to Aleppo. The army was deployed and the weights and the equipment were taken to the rear of the army. The Sultan's household troops were given their armor and weapons; thus, everyone was armed. The Ottoman army resembled "an iron sea" from a distance. That soldiers needed to move forward with their weapons, made the trek very difficult. In the meantime, the news about the conquest of the Besni Castle arrived.

Yavuz Sultan sent Al-Ghawri a very harsh letter. In the letter he said: "We act for the revitalization of the Islamic law and we don't have any secret agenda. However, you help nonbelievers. Thus, your enmity becomes obvious. For this reason, our imperial military campaign is directed to you; we are moving towards you in your country by getting your cities. Now we are camping in Tucak Creek. If it looks easy to you and if you have just a little bit of patriotism, you should be ready for a battle no matter in wherever or in whatever condition."

The army came close to Antep. Here the military camp was established and a council meeting was held to discuss the battle strategy until the Maghrib Prayer. On the same day, soldiers worked on the battle tactics by practicing among themselves. Battle preparations lasted the next day as well and regiments were ordered one last time. Food was distributed.

A spy coming on the third day in Antep brought news that the Egyptian Sultan exited Aleppo and was waiting at the Marj Dabiq Plain where the tomb of Prophet David was located. Then, due to the possibility of a night raid, most of the soldiers slept on their horses. The rest of the soldiers slept with their guns.

TWO ARMIES AT THE PITCHED
BATTLE OF MARJ DABIQ

The forces meeting at the Marj Dabiq plain were equivalent in number. Almost all of the Mamluk army consisted of cavalry; they did not have fire power and they were equipped with cutting and piercing weapons. The Egyptian army relied on their good horses and qualified armored mounted troops. They knew that the Ottomans had firearms; however, they thought that these weapons worked in fortress siege situations, but they would not have an effect in a pitched battle. They thought that firearms could not do anything against cavalry attacks, which would be made by spreading over a wide area. The most important point the Mamluks missed was the ability of the Ottoman infantries armed with guns to change their location and make a collective attack. This delinquency would have been the biggest reason for them to lose the war.

The Ottoman side was composed of approximately 65,000 soldiers. There were 8,000 janissaries and mounted troops were following them in number. Twenty thousand Anatolian Timar holders and 20,000 Rumelian

Timar holders were at the Sultan's side. As reserve forces, the forces of local governors joined the Ottoman army and they numbered about 8,000–10,000. Among janissaries whose primary duties were to protect the Sultan in war and in peace, there were about 2,000 musketeers and about 2,000 archers.

Although various numbers were given in the sources for the number of cannons, in reality, the army had about 150 cannons. It is quite likely that the reason for choosing the light cannons is because of the length of the road and the big cannons were slowing down the army in these kinds of walks.

On Sunday, the 24th of August, 1516, immediately after the Fajr Prayer, the Ottomans on the battlefield took a classical battle order. In the center of the order was the Sultan. The Sultan was surrounded by mercenaries and there were cavalry soldiers on his right, and on their right side there were armored cavalrymen of janissaries and the *garip yiğitler* ("the forlorn brave men") on the Sultan's left. There were cavalrymen of janissaries on the left, and the *garip yiğitler* on the left. In front of the janissaries, janissaries were lined up with their guns and bows and artillerymen were located on their left. To defend janissaries and to make them use their guns comfortably, Anatolian soldiers with lances stood on their left and Rumelian soldiers stood on their right. In front of the janissaries armed with guns, there were artillerymen, and moreover, the weapons of the army were brought here. The center was protected by light cannons interconnected with chains and troops armed with guns, as well as herds of camels. It was as strong as the wall of a castle.

On both sides of the forces at the center were the soldiers of the governor generals of Anatolia and Rumelia as well as local troops made up of Kurdish governors. The formation was not back to back but side by side. The bird's eye view of the army showed a shape like a crescent.

Yavuz Sultan Selim Khan exclaimed to his soldiers right before the war: "My dear soldiers! Now is the time, let me see your maximum efforts." These words encouraged the soldiers even more. The Sultan stopped to pray for the success of his soldiers.

He even writes in the *Selimşahname* that they hid the fast-mounted troops like an ambush and started their first abrasive attack with them. The battle started first with short strokes of the frontier soldiers and a simultaneous fusillade of Ottoman cannons to scare the opponent.

The encountering Ottoman and Mamluk armies did not attack each other right away. They stopped for a while and tried to understand their opponent's power.

At the beginning of the war, because the Mamluks knew the firepower of the Ottomans, they did not enter a range of the weapons and tried to draw the attention of Ottoman soldiers by fooling around on their horses with a variety of shows. Their goal was to stay away from the center of the Ottoman army and hit it from the sides to make their way toward the back. Thus, they would have ensured their security by staying away from the center where the cannons and guns were located and they would have made their way toward the back by gradual harassing raids on the sides. In the sources of that era, it is mentioned that the Mamluk army aimed to panic the Ottoman troops by making their way through the sides of the army to disperse and disrupt the order. Thus they would have dispersed the lines of the Ottoman soldiers. They started the first devastating attack from the right wing with their fast cavalry. The sequential artillery shootings of the Ottoman cannons to scare the enemy left them surrounded by gunpowder smoke.

The Mamluk cavalry attacked the very end of the Ottomans' right wing at the moment when the visual range was very limited due to the smoke. Other Mamluk forces joined them. A fierce cavalry battle had started on the Ottomans' right wing. On the other hand, the Ottomans' left wing was opposing the weak Mamluk attacks. At these first collisions, there was wavering on the Ottoman wings. At the most ardent moment of the war, Sinan Pasha and Yunus Pasha were transferred to the right and left wings, respectively. They had the cavalry of the Sultan's household troops as well as gun-smith infantries with them.

Sultan Selim Khan, sending soldiers to reinforce the wings, was bawling at his soldiers with all of his power: "Today is the day of effort and patriotism and nobody can escape from death. One cannot get away from death by escaping. If martyrdom is granted to us, the happiness in the hereafter is ours or if we crush the enemy, the state in this world is ours. It is the time of patriotism, let's show our efforts…" The effect of these words was understood when the reinforcement soldiers secured the stability of the wings.

While the cavalry collisions continued at the right and left wings, the Sultan pushed the janissaries located at the center forward along with the artillery and gun fire towards the center of Mamluks; the endless noises of the guns and artilleries roared. The gun carriages were transversely driven in a way that they would not block each other and the foot soldiers armed with guns were moving forward beside them by providing the continuity of the fire. This resembles the contemporary strategy of infantry forces moving forward by using the tanks as shields during land occupations. The center of the Mamluks' force fell apart in a short time. Yavuz Sultan Selim also commanded the foot and mounted soldiers on the right and left to move forward.

The sudden move of the center branch of the Ottoman army dispersed the attacking Mamluks using the hit and run tactic, and even though they desperately performed minor assaults, these couldn't go further than some minor setbacks. Gun and artillery shooting of the Ottoman central forces caused even the soldiers next to Al-Ghawri to flee.

AFTER THE BATTLE OF MARJ DABIQ

The Egyptian historian Ibn Zunbul, evaluating the battle from the Mamluks' perspective, describes the Battle of Marj Dabiq as follows: "Those fighting against the Ottomans at Marj Dabiq were about 2,000 Circassians. Other Mamluk forces couldn't even enter the battle due to their fear. At the beginning of the war, it was not certain who was going to attack and who was going to stay on the defensive in the Egyptian army. A big crisis broke out on this issue. The discipline of the Mamluk army was ruined during the war, but there was no contention among the Ottoman forces. Each soldier knew what to do and moved altogether with strict discipline. Also, Sultan Selim came up to the middle ranks of the army galloping on his horse during the war.

The Sultan was holding Umar's sword, constantly praising his soldiers and encouraging his commanders. The army, seeing their Sultan beside them, streamed upon Mamluks."

The main conflict of the Battle of Marj Dabiq lasted about three hours and the battle was entirely over when the time of the *Asr* (Afternoon) Prayer has been reached. The battle was also a victory of the Ottomans' dispassionateness and not compromising in their combat discipline. No matter what happened, the army strictly obeyed their orders and never panicked.

The central forces usually, responsible to preserve the center and the headquarters of the army, changed the course of the battle completely at Marj Dabiq. The Ottomans lined up at the battlefield as usual; however, they won the battle in an unusual way. This shows that the Ottomans had the discipline and skills capable to make sudden tactical changes based on the offensiveness of the other side.

Al-Ghawri died falling from a horse after the war. Yet after the war, the Sultan compliments the Caliph who came with the Mamluks and put a robe of honor on him and then took him to Cairo with him.

As a result of Marj Dabiq victory, not only Syria, Lebanon, and Palestine fall under domination of Ottoman Empire, but also a major step was taken for the conquest of Egypt. The politics that the Sultan followed after the victory was the operation of obtaining the big cities in the region. The Sultan was hesitant about going further than that.

The ancient weapons and armors
displayed at the Ottoman Military Museum

At the first council meeting after the war, the Sultan asked about the situation in Aleppo. Precisely during this period, one of the viziers, Yunus Pasha, met the Aleppo chief of Mamluks, Hayırbey, and brought him to the Sultan's side. Hayırbey said that Mamluks went to Hama and Hums and they were having conflicts and arguments about who was going to be the Sultan. Afterwards, he declared his obedience and thus for the first time a Mamluk commander entered the service of the Ottomans.

In their letter, the Aleppo community, referring to the Mamluks, asked Sultan Selim to clear their city from Circassian and Turkmen people. In the letter, it was said "...protecting us from Circassian people is like protecting us from the hands of infidels." Following the victory, the first city to go was Aleppo and people obeyed without resistance.

Yavuz Sultan Selim entered Aleppo on the 28th of August, 1516, and stayed in the city for two weeks. A sermon was delivered in his name and he made various appointments for the city. In the region named 'Arabian City' by the Ottomans, sanjaks were created and new appointments were made for each sanjak. Baalbek, Hama, Hums, Sis, Tripoli, Birecik, and Tarsus were connected to the Ottomans.

He sent the soldiers of Diyarbekir Main Principality and Kurdish tribal forces, which had come to help the army in case of a possible attack of Safavids, back to their hometown to spend the winter. This activity was showing that not the conquest of Egypt, but rather the elimination of the danger of Shah Ismail was the Sultan's goal.

The Sultan held a council meeting for the first time in Aleppo and discussed his military plan with his viziers, commanders, and scholars. He expressed his thoughts about marching towards Damascus. The intelligence that the notables held a meeting in Damascus and planned to attack the Ottomans after electing a Sultan among themselves was discussed in this meeting. Al-Ghawri's son, Muhammad, and Canberdi Gazali were fighting to become the Sultan of Mamluks. In addition, the topics of the safety of the pilgrimage road and the people living on the Holy Land, Mecca and Medina, and rescuing them from the tyranny of the Mamluks, were discussed. People in the council supported the idea of marching towards Damascus. Even though the essential part of the army was sent back to where they had previously been stationed, it was decided to continue the expedition.

The Sultan also sent a messenger to Istanbul and ordered that the ships should be ready and the Ottoman navy should set sail for the Mediterranean Sea.

YAVUZ IS IN DAMASCUS

H e prepared thousands of lyster bags to avoid the thirst on the road before setting off towards Damascus. The Sultan had started to march with 12,000 soldiers of the Sultan's household troops. First of all, he came to Hama and first thing he did was to visit the tomb of Imam Zeynelabidin, located at a high place and prayed there. He arrived at Hums after two days and Damascus after three days; however, he did not enter the city and waited for the maintenance of public order. He entered Damascus after twelve days.

At the first council meeting in Damascus, he declared that previous Mamluk practices were repealed and he made some appointments. The next day, he had the Anatolian and Rumelian soldiers counted and appointed them to winter quarters, which meant that the Egypt expedition had ended.

One of the first things Yavuz had done when coming to Damascus was search for the tomb of Muhyiddin ibn Arabi. The great scholar, Muhyiddin ibn Arabi, who made substantial influence on the history of

Sufism and Islamic thought, also affected the Ottoman mysticism deeply with his thoughts. It is said that the mentor of Osman Ghazi, Sheikh Edebali, received lessons from Ibn Arabi in Damascus. Moreover, that the commentator Davud-i Kayseri, the first head teacher of the Ottomans, gave lectures to others using the Ibn Arabi's work and that Davud-i Kayseri's student Molla Fenari, the first Sheikh al-Islam, shows the deep connection between the Ottomans and Ibn Arabi. However, this great scholar had not been appreciated enough by that period's government and his tomb was destroyed and abolished.

He also said before his death that his tomb would be destroyed and added that when the "sin" enters the "shin," the tomb of Muhyiddin would emerge. Even though a relationship was not established between the letters of "sin" and "shin" in the alphabet and the discovery of his tomb in that period, it was understood afterwards that the letter "sin" was the first letter of the Ottoman Sultan Selim and the letter "shin" was the first letter of Sham (Damascus). The expression of "when the 'sin' enters the 'shin' implies the entrance of the Sultan to this ancient city; thus, at the time of Sultan Selim, the tomb of this famous Sufi scholar was found. The Sultan ordered a shrine to be built at the place that had been found. There is not clear information about how the tomb was found, however, Evliya Çelebi says in his *Seyahatname* that the Sultan sees

Muhyiddin ibn Arabi in his dream and in the dream Arabi tells the Sultan to ride a black horse that will find his tomb. Upon this, in the morning, Yavuz does what he was told to do, and the horse paws the earth in the dump, and the Sultan finds the tombstone by himself when he digs at this place.

WHETHER THERE WILL BE
AN EXPEDITION TO EGYPT
OR NOT

The Sultan performed his first Friday Prayer in Damascus at the Umayyad Mosque, a sermon was delivered on his behalf, and then he went to see the Qur'an attributed to Uthman, and he also visited the place where Prophet Jesus will descend close to the apocalypse. In addition, he wandered around in many sacred places in Damascus.

The Sultan, wishing to meet Sheikh Muhammad Bedahṣi, a great scholar and opinion leader of that period who was staying in the Umayyad Mosque, did not call the Sheikh to come see him, but rather, he went to visit him.

He sat quietly with perfect politeness in the presence of the Sheikh. The Sheikh was quiet as well. This silence continued for a period of time. For Ottomans, in which the number of spoken words per minute is counted, chatter is considered to be shameful.

The Umayyad Mosque in Damascus

When the Sultan's chief physician, Ahi Çelebi, noticed the silence and started talking about the weather in Damascus, the Sultan didn't like this empty talk. He silenced the chief physician by giving him a black look and asked the Sheikh for a helpful prayer. As for the Sheikh, he showed humility and said that he himself asked for a prayer since the Sultan is the foundation of all Muslims.

Upon Sultan Selim asking for a prayer insistently, he also made a prayer. They separated by bidding farewell to each other.

One night the Sultan saw the Sheikh in his dream when he arrived at Cairo. He wore a shepherd's felt cloak, the one he wore when he met him. Hasan Can, to whom the Sultan told his dream, interprets it as the death of the Sheikh. The Sovereign knew very well that dreams should be interpreted in a good way. He became angry at Hasan Can, and told him that the realization of the dream would be with his interpretation and if anything happens to the Sheikh, he would connect that to his interpretation and he would deserve a punishment. Hasan Can became very sad about this situation. When Halimi Çelebi came to see the Sultan the next day, he told him that Hasan Can deserved punishment, and he made a mistake interpreting the dream, and if anything happened to the Sheikh, he would blame him.

Hasan Can asked that the night the Sultan had the dream should be identified and if anything happened to the Sheikh, it should be determined if it happened before or after the interpretation so that he would deserve punishment or benevolence accordingly.

The Sultan declared that there was a way to do that, and he instantly wrote the date on a paper with his own hand. After a couple of days, messengers come from Damascus and reports that the Sheikh was dead. The Sheikh said in his last breath that the people of Damascus should submit to the Sultan since God sent him, and he saved them from the hands of Circassian. He also asked them to convey his greetings and prayers to the Sultan. In addition, he wrote a letter of testament full of advice to be delivered to the Sultan.

When the letter was delivered to the Sultan in his pavilion, he immediately called Halimi Effendi inside. Afterwards, he turned to Hasan Can and reproached him by saying that due to his interpretation that good-natured saint was now dead.

Then, Hasan Can curiously asked about the day of his death. The Sultan gave him the letter with a laugh. After their calculations, Hasan Can and Halimi Effendi determined that the night of the death and the dream fit. Hasan Can deserved benevolence. Hasan Can also interpreted this story for the Sultan's sainthood and said that his dream became true exactly as it was.

While Yavuz Sultan Selim was in Damascus, it snowed and the weather got cold. This situation was interpreted as good tidings that during the prospective challenging expedition, the road conditions would be acceptable.

The Sultan spoke to Idris Bitlisi and Grand Vizier Sinan Pasha. He asked the opinions of the highest ranked statesmen about whether to march or not to march on Cairo. While the Sultan Selim was thinking about the new campaign, soldiers, on the other hand, were tired of being on the road for campaigns.

In Damascus, soldiers started to ask about why they didn't go back since the battle is over. They started to criticize their being continuously lodged in new cities and said: "We don't stay at the same place for a couple of days; which Sultan deemed this torture proper for his soldiers." These rumors even reached the Sultan's ears.

Sultan Selim acknowledged the soldiers' complaints and said he intended for them to go back. However, he saw it as essential to keep track of the current state for a while to learn the news coming from Cairo.

As for Mamluks, the next head of the state became the subject of debate. With the alliance of the leaders, it was decided that Tumanbay, whom Al-Ghawri left as vicegerent in place of himself, would be the Mamluk Sultan. Sultan Selim's hesitations about marching towards Cairo increased when hearing of it.

The Sultan discussed this issue with Idris Bitlisi at length. Idris Bitlisi says in his book that the Sultan sent a caravan to the Haramayn (Mecca and Medina) about this issue; meanwhile, Devatdar Tumanbay was made a Sultan and while these things were happening, Mamluks handed the Hejaz Path in to bandits of the city. He said that the Ottomans were sure that Egyptians could not give the Ottomans a hard time since the Egyptian path is covered in the desert with no water. The Mamluks said: "None of the conquerors tried this way."

Meanwhile, the month of Ramadan came and the Sultan, statesmen, and soldiers start their fast in Damascus.

Among the commanders, there were serious discussions about going on the military campaign and concerns were expressed.

Commanders thought that it would be difficult for the army to gather in a place far from the Ottoman territories and expressed their hesitation about the risks of entering such a dangerous battle with the limited number of elite soldiers, versus a crowded army such as the Egyptian army. They thought that carrying food, beverages, and water in the vast desert was impossible and they said that the destination was far away.

In those days, there was an unusual debate in the Ottoman council. When the Anatolian Head Governor Zeynel Pasha and the Anatolian Head of the Financial Department Zehrimar Kasım Effendi started to argue in front of the Sultan about the preparations of the prospective campaign, everyone watched them in a daze. Not allowing this disrespectfulness to continue any further, the Sultan dismissed them from their positions and appointed other officials in their place.

This tactlessness at the council in front of the Sultan can be seen as another outbreak of the current tension in the army and it revealed the distress and concerns in the army.

Discussions concentrated on the shortage of the available troops, troubles in obtaining logistical support, and climate conditions, and it was verbalized that these serious issues might cause a great defeat.

On the other hand, Yavuz Sultan Selim was not willing to lose the advantages gained with Marj Dabiq with the reorganization of the Mamluks. Trusting the incoming intelligence that there was no unity and solidarity in the Egyptian army, he thought that he could overcome them easily; thus, he decided to march towards Cairo. He asked the opinion of Şehsuvaroğlu Ali Bey who was originally from Dulkadirids Principality, but later entered under the Ottoman service.

Şehsuvaroğlu explained that just as the Sultan headed for Azerbaijan, he entered Mamluk country and he needed to keep this country under his control as Mamluk resistance was not broken and they had chosen a new Sultan. On the other hand, Hayırbey, one of former Mamluk rulers entering the Ottoman service, said that the inability to capture the whole of Egypt would be beneath the Sultan and the Haramayn was in need of service.

Thoughtful Yavuz Sultan Selim said: "I know all of this but I also know that Timur fights against Egypt Sultan Berkuk. Moreover, I know the deserts on the path of Cairo and I know that Timur came all the way up to Damascus but he doesn't march towards Cairo." Upon the Sultan's speech, Hayırbey commented: "Your Excellency! However the way Mamluk soldiers passed through the desert with their very crowded army, your highness can pass with that much easiness, God willing."

Cairo

The Sultan agreed with these words and gave up about his idea of returning completely. In response to Hayırbey's insistence on marching towards Egypt, the Grand Vizier Sinan Pasha gave an opinion that a military campaign was not a good idea based on the facts that they should be content with the region of Damascus starting from Gaza, since, if a defeat occurred after attempting to fight against Mamluks, the army would never be safe and the Arab tribes in the region should also be taken into account.

At the council meeting, due to the opposition of the viziers and the military judges about the military campaign, it was decided that diplomatic ways should be used before the military campaign:

"Mamluks declaring someone named Tumanbay as the Sultan after fleeing from Damascus and coming to Egypt want to fight again. Now let's write a letter and invite him. If he accepts the invitation and shows obedience, we shall hand his country to him again and we will return to our land. If he doesn't accept, we will take measures accordingly."

Upon this decision, a letter was written and sent to Tumanbay via three envoys.

In the letter, the Sultan gave Tumanbay several pieces of advices. The Sultan added in his letter that the ownership of the region belonged to him by right of conquest, he didn't plead to the Caliph and judges like him, he became the Sultan by taking over the reign from his father, he needed to send the tax of Egypt annually like it had been done previously for Baghdad Caliphs, he was superior to him because he was "the shadow of God" on Earth and the servant of the Haramayn.

A similar letter was sent to Canberdi Ghazali accompanying Tumanbay. In that letter, it was mentioned that they trusted Canberdi. It was mentioned clearly that he did not reply to the letter written by the viziers previously, but if he submitted to them, he and whichever Emir coming along with him would be treated nicely.

Yavuz Selim Khan was inviting Tumanbay to be his subject to him and if it happened that way he was guaranteeing him fair treatment; however if he was not faithful to the promise, he would be punished.

In some sources it stated that the letter proposed that in return to a sermon to be read on behalf of the Sultan, money to be released and a tribute to be paid, the region from Gaza to Egypt would have been left under the administration of Tumanbay.

The letter was based on the idea that Tumanbay would stay as an administrator in Egypt under the governance of the Ottomans, annexing Egypt to the Ottomans.

The preparations in Damascus started. Upon Canberdi Ghazali's march from Cairo to Gaza with 5,000 soldiers, troops were dispatched to the region. In addition, the Grand Vizier Sinan Pasha set out from Damascus with reinforcement troops. The first units who arrived captured Gaza easily.

At the council meeting held a few days later, the subject of a military campaign against Cairo was discussed at length. According to citations of Idris Bitlisi witnessing that period, Pashas were saying:

"It is difficult this winter for the army to recover and gather in remote areas far from the Ottoman lands. How is that possible to start and win such a dangerous military campaign against a very large Egyptian army by using elites and the adjacent soldiers who are currently in service? For this reason, it seems impossible for the food and beverage items to be loaded on camels and carried through the never-ending desert with no water and grass; the destination is too far away."

Viziers were partially right in their concerns. The number of available soldiers was lower than desired, and the logistical support needed for the army, and the extreme climate could have caused serious trouble and insurmountable trials and hardships for the army of Yavuz Sultan Selim.

The Sultan's opinion was very different. He wanted to collect the fruits of an already earned victory. If the enemy was allowed respite, they would have found an opportunity to recover and all the gains achieved by the Ottomans would have been endangered.

The news about the messy state of the Egyptian army after Marj Dabiq and low possibility that they could have achieved unity among themselves was comforting to the Sultan. The Sultan, relying on the arriving intelligence, insisted on his decision about fighting against Egypt to completely eliminate the Mamluks, thinking that it would not be difficult to beat the Egyptian army again.

The preparations were accelerated. Treasures were mounted on camels purchased for this purpose. To increase the motivation of the soldiers, trimonthly salaries were increased and plenty of tips were distributed. The artillery started test shots after doing maintenance work on the cannons outside of Damascus. A messenger coming from Istanbul gave news to the Sultan that the navy was waiting for a command to move, and the peace treaty done with the Hungarians was renewed. The Sultan was glad of the news.

An order had been given to the chief admiral Cafer Bey previously about the preparation of the navy; the chief admiral had quickly tried to complete the necessary preparations; however, the navy couldn't have moved just in time due to the harsh winter. After the preparations were made, a total of 106 ships could set out from Istanbul on the 26th of March.

Sultan Selim was waiting for the support coming from the sea after arriving at Gaza. However, even if things did not go as planned due to the delay, following the news coming from Istanbul, they headed from Damascus to Gaza in three days. Another enemy worrying the Sultan other than the Hungarians was Shah Ismail. However, the news coming about the Shah was showing that he had not become a threat for the Ottomans yet.

Yavuz Sultan Selim sent his letter mentioned above four days after leaving Damascus. In addition, letters written by Hayırbey and the Ottoman viziers were also sent to Canberdi and other Emirs.

Mamluk ruler Tumanbay, relieved when he received the letter, accepted the Ottoman administration to be accepted everywhere and that he would be the Egyptian regent.

One of the Mamluk emirs, Emir Allan, informed about the news, immediately ran towards the palace of

Tumanbay. When he saw the three envoys waiting in the palace, he killed them at once.

He angrily appeared in front Tumanbay and asked him if he had accepted the demands of the Ottoman Sultan. Tumanbay said in meaning: "I don't want to cause the shedding of blood of Muslims. I wish that everybody stays in their homeland and if we don't do that, we will encounter danger. The commanders and emirs in our army are in competition, none of them trusts one another. My wish is that the Mamluk state would not be fully extinct, and for this reason I will accept their offer."

Emir Allan was trying to convince Tumanbay and said: "I fought against the Ottomans at Marj Dabiq and I got to know them pretty well. I saw with my own eyes that they can never ride horses and use weapons like Mamluk cavalry soldiers. Their only trick is the cannons and guns. Their infantry used firearms. They don't know the science of war. We can crush them easily under our horses' feet by attacking the enemy's infantry-men with all of our cavalrymen. We will win the battle by taking the Sultan captive."

As a result of long pursuits, Emir Allan managed to convince both Tumanbay and other emirs who had already taken a dim view of the war. History had a lot of rulers scoring historic failures by following the insis-tence of their subordinates instead of applying their own ideas and Tumanbay also became one of those rulers, misled by some of their advisors. The brand new ruler of Egypt consented to fight against the Ottomans while once he did not want to cause the shedding of Muslim blood.

BATTLE IN GAZA

T umanbay had difficulties establishing an army as well since emirs found the money offered insufficient. Then the Sultan told them there was not even a penny at the treasury so they should go and fight for themselves and their families. He also added that he himself was also one of them and if they went to fight he would go with them; if not, he would not go as well. He could manage to gather the soldiers at last. Seeing that emirs were ready to fight, he dispatched the forces that consisted of some of the major emirs under the commandment of Canberdi.

The purpose of the units under the commandment of Canberdi advancing towards Gaza was to wear the Ottoman army out by intercepting them on their path, to prevent them from finding provisions and to block the Cairo route.

In the Battle of Gaza, the Ottoman forces under the commandment of Grand Vizier Sinan Pasha heavily defeated Canberdi Ghazali's units by using a clever tactic. Canberdi lost one third of his forces.

While the Battle of Gaza meant breaking the resistance and ruining morale on the Mamluks' side, it meant just the opposite on the other side; in other words, it strengthened the spirituality of the Ottomans. There was only one enemy left in front of them up to Cairo, which was the long route in the desert. They knew very well that the water shortage that comes with being in the desert would cause a great danger for the Ottoman army.

An Ottoman matchlock musket

The Sultan was very happy about the victory at Gaza because it was pointing to an irreversible path they had just entered. As he was moving forward to Gaza being concerned about military threats, he was also planning to visit the Holy places in Cairo.

YAVUZ IS IN JERUSALEM

When the Sultan expressed his wish about visiting Cairo, statesmen said that it would be more appropriate to do it after the military campaign, due to security measures. Upon this, Idris Bitlisi, who had encouraged the Sultan for this visit, told him that according to the virtual and spiritual reign, the right to be the Sultan of the Holy Land belongs to the Prophet Solomon (upon him be peace) and Prophet Dawud, peace be upon him, based on a hadith he mentioned: "Only three masjids reinforce people which are Masjid al-Aqsa, Masjid al-Haram, and my Masjid." He stated that the powerful Sultans are the successors of Prophet Muhammad, peace and blessings be upon him, and other Prophets; for this reason, it is not appropriate to pass by without visiting the Holy Places while being so close to them; it is befitted for Sultans to show honor and respect to their predecessors. Receiving the news that they had been victorious in the Battle of Gaza, the Sultan decided to do the visitation. He arrived at Jerusalem under the protection of 500 musketeers and about 1,000 of the Sultan's household cavalrymen protecting him.

He set up a tent as he always used to do before entering every new city. He relaxed there for a while and by sending a message to the officials at the Masjid al-Aqsa, he informed them that he would perform the Maghrib Prayer in there. Feridun Emecen, writing about the Jerusalem visit of the Sultan based on the sources of that period, reports this visit as follows: "Then he came in front of the Dome of the Rock, dismounted and visited this place first. After walking fifty-five steps he reached the stairs, and then climbed up with fifteen steps, so he came in front of its door with a total sixty steps. After visiting Prophet Dawud's prayer place, he walked around the *Sakhra* (the Foundation Stone), went down thirteen steps below, and performed the Hajah Prayer. Walking out of there, he again performed Prayers and recited supplications in front of the *mihrab* on the left side of the Foundation Stone).

Then he came out and gave plenty of tips to the workers at this place. Again by walking down the *sahre*, he passed through the courtyard with one hundred and fifty steps and reached the Masjid al-Aqsa. The servants welcomed him by holding candles in their hands.

He reached the front of the mihrab at eighty-five steps, performed the Maghrib Prayer, then after the Prayer he visited gigantic columns on both sides of the *mihrab*, stayed there a little while; afterwards, he came in front of the mihrab again and performed the Hajah

Prayer, engaged in '*dhikr* and recitation,' and prayed. After he finished praying, he performed the Isha Prayer, and again he distributed many tips to the workers.

Jerusalem

After exiting the mosque, he got on his horse and his men accompanied him by lighting lanterns and torches. That night, he stayed in the pavilion located outside of the city. The next morning, he ordered a great number of animals to be slaughtered and their meat to be distributed to the poor.

By getting on his horse, he visited the Dome of the Rock in the daylight this time, prayed two units of the Hajah Prayer in the Masjid al-Aqsa and after then he walked around the places in Jerusalem. Idris Bitlisi, at this point, narrates that the Sultan visited the graves of the Prophets Isaac, Jacob, and Joseph; not only did he recite the Qur'an, but he also made Isfahani Mehmed Effendi recite the Qur'an. Afterwards, he granted charity and beneficence to the people of Jerusalem without the discrimination of religion.

Yavuz Sultan Selim with the drawing of Levni

FROM JERUSALEM TO CAIRO

I t was a great mercy that it was winter. While in Damascus, it snowed and they proceeded towards Jerusalem under the rain, so there wasn't any lack of water, which had been feared.

Yavuz Sultan Selim Khan interpreted all of these as a sign of God's grace to His servants.

While considering what to do with thirst, following the rain was interpreted as a Divine sign. However, there were still some Pashas protesting the battle and they did not want to go beyond Gaza.

The Sultan arrived in Gaza on the 2nd of January, 1517, and he met the Grand Vizier Sinan Pasha there. He visited the Halilurrahman. He completed the last preparations of the Egypt military campaign in Gaza.

He sent Sinan Pasha and Hayırbey on ahead to provide security. In a meeting, Yavuz was very angry with Hüseyin Pasha one of the pashas still spreading the idea of returning by bringing up the difficulty of the road and lack of military.

The pasha was continuously talking about the hardship of the military campaign and requesting that the invasion of Egypt be ended.

Being aware that the Pasha's ideas were spreading among soldiers, he was concerned that this would cause unrest in the army.

He punished Hüseyin Pasha most severely to make an example for those who thought about going back after the decision of military campaign had already been made. This issue was never brought up again.

Passing through the Katya Desert was part of a specific plan. By sending pioneers on the route to Cairo, the places the army would stay were determined. From Gaza to Salihiyye, eight places were chosen.

The Sultan left Gaza on January 9th and arrived in Arish on the 11th of January. The rain they had while passing through the most difficult part of the desert was not quenching their thirst but also making the walking easier because it was firming up the sand.

Sultan Selim was one of the Sultans knowing that God helps those on the right path. Although there was a partial water shortage after Arish, they did not encounter big issues except for the trouble of gun carriages getting stuck in the sand. This problem was also solved by putting more animals on the carriages to move them.

The most difficult part of the road was passed through much more easily than they had expected. It is narrated that during this march, the Sultan dismounted at one stage and after seeing this, the army also dismounted and walked in the desert and then when he got on his horse again he was asked why he did this way and he answered as "How can we ride our horses while our blessed Prophet, peace and blessing be upon him, walks in front of us?"

Along the way, the attacks by the desert Arabs annoyed the Ottomans. These attacks aimed at looting on one hand, and on the other hand, they aimed to save time for Tumanbey. The Ottoman army, starting to get annoyed by these attacks, began to take them seriously and prepared the military at their stop in Hanka. Against a Bedouin attack, Sinan Pasha, Hayırbey, Dulkadirli Şehsuvaroğlu Ali Bey, and Ramazanoğlu Mahmud Bey prepared an ambush at night and the real surprise was for those coming to attack. Bedouins tried to prevent the soldiers to get water by besieging the well at the next place they stopped the following day, so Sinan Pasha disrupted the siege some artillery shooting; however, at that moment, there was a huge mobilization in the Ottoman army.

As soon as Mamluk soldiers appeared at their accommodations, the army formed ranks and Yavuz jumped on his horse. After soldiers got into battle formation, it was seen that the alarm was irrelevant and the number of Mamluk soldiers were not enough to be able to cause a danger. As a matter of fact, they had already run off when they had seen the Ottomans.

Meanwhile, the state of the military was revised and the number of the Ottoman soldiers was detected as 20,000. This number was less than expected for a pitched battle. However, Yavuz Sultan Selim Khan trusted his army and commanders.

In the meantime, an unseen war, which had been taking place among spies, had already started a long time ago. The spies of Tumanbay were collecting intelligence about the Ottoman army.

The spies, entering the army in vendor costumes, were carrying information to Egypt about the number of Ottoman soldiers and the situation of their weapons. Yavuz Selim Khan also was using a similar method and he was determining his strategy he would follow against the Mamluks according to the upcoming intelligence.

Yavuz Sultan Selim Khan

THE OTTOMANS AGAINST
EGYPT CIRCASSIANS

While Yavuz Selim Khan was preparing for the battle with an army of 20,000 Ottoman soldiers, Tumanbay was making preparations with the same number of soldiers at Salihiyye where the Ottomans would emerge from the desert. According to his plan, a surprise attack against the tired Ottoman army by not letting them rest would have been more effective. Emirs were not in agreement with Tumanbay; according to them, the Ottoman army was already used to defense wars and an attack would not have been beneficial. To confuse the Ottomans, they needed to establish a defense line and wait for their enemy there.

When Tumanbay heard that the Ottomans came to Hanke, he agreed upon building a front line at Ridaniya in front of Cairo to prevent the upcoming army after negotiating with emirs. Trenches were excavated from Mount al-Mukattam to the Nile River to stop the Ottoman army. The defense line took two months to complete. The cannons at the castles were brought and the guns were moved to the defense line. One of the big cannons was buried under the sand as well. Assistance for the supply and usage of the cannons was obtained from the European states. The giant cannon, as well as the other cannons, and the guns would surprise the Ottoman army with salvo bombing. The cavalry would attack the Ottoman army, welcomed and surprised by the cannons, and those coming from Anatolia would be defeated, falling into a trap in a land they did not know at all. The Mamluks' plan showed on paper that victory was guaranteed; however, history had witnessed that plans on paper and reality can give very different results. Afterwards, everyone waited for the battle.

In the intelligence the Ottomans received, there was some information about the defense decision Tumanbay made after his consultation with the emirs, defense lines and the firearms placed on these lines. Those who were loyal to Hayırbey, one of the previous emirs of Mamluks entering Ottoman service, met the Ottomans' need for intelligence. The creation of the action plan was based on the recommendations of Hayırbey, who knew the area very well.

The Ottomans' battle strategy changed again according to the position of the enemy. According to the plan, the army wouldn't attack the front line where the cannons were located directly; instead, it would roam around the mountain from the back to attack the Mamluks. When the army arrived at Birkatu'l-Haj, a brief clash occurred and then Circassian troops appeared. After a consultation with his viziers, Yavuz told them: "What should we do? Time is running out. When the battle starts, it will possibly continue until night and the situation would be different." It was decided that the military camp would be established at the meeting place and military cargo would be moved to the back against a possible attack.

The army spent the night under stress. The troops got ready the next morning and common military arrangements were prepared. The main troops were still at the center; the mounted troops on both sides were proceeding by protecting the center. On the right and left wings, there were soldiers of Evrenos and Mihal-oğulları, two of Rumelia's margraves.

THE PITCHED BATTLE OF RIDANIYA

Because the Egyptian army was planning to encounter the enemy from the front line, the cavalry units (Cundi) were showing themselves off in front of the Ottomans and trying to attract them. Tumanbay was keeping two of his emirs next to himself, and he was watching for the big starboard showing the location of the Sultan, and was waiting to act according to the Ottoman attack. When the starboard had been seen and if they had had a chance, their highly skilled riders would have attacked there directly and shot the Ottoman army right in the heart.

Since they never had done this before, they did not have an exact idea about how they would do the cavalry attack along with the artillery shooting. The hussars were worried that the artillery shooting would harm them before the Ottomans.

Egyptians did not think about the possibility that the Ottomans would come from the mountain side, so they did not have any military precautions for that.

The Ottoman army started to proceed from the front line and while they were approaching the Mamluk cannons, they marched towards Mount al-Mukattam by turning left just before entering the artillery range. The small units in the front distracted Mamluks with momentary first clashes, and this tactic demonstrated the success of Yavuz Sultan Selim's strong intelligence network. This sudden maneuver by the Ottomans turned all military plans of Mamluks upside down. The Egyptian army panicked. The artillery remained idle; even if they tried to direct the cannons fixed in the sand to the Ottomans, it was not possible in this panicked environment. The lines fell out of order. They took the cannons from where they were placed, turned on the carriages and turned. To do all of this, they needed to get out of their trenches that they had dug. It wasn't even possible to turn the heavy cannons stuck in the sand. These cannons obtained from the cavalry of Rhodes and that they had set their hopes on did not do the job at all.

At the very moment when the Mamluk army got out of their trenches and came up front with the light cannons they had succeeded to turn, the Ottomans bombarded the Mamluk side with their own cannons they had brought by pulling all the way. The cannons fired all together messed up the Mamluk fortifications and concentrations.

While the janissary musketeers descended from the mountain, gun shots rang out. The Mamluks found time neither to gather strength nor to use the cannons. In the sources from that era, it was narrated that the gunpowder smoke coming out of the cannons and guns sparked by the Ottomans left everyone under a dark fog. The first phase of the battle finished.

The second phase started when the Mamluks organized their lines and the two armies started mutual attacks at Ridaniya Sahara. Before the Mamluks managed to put the balls in the cannons so they could be brought to the right side, the Rumelian units of the Ottomans' left arm started to attack. Meanwhile, one of the Mamluk artillerymen escaped after making only one shot. The wrecking ball dropped in the middle of the Ottoman soldiers. Yavuz Sultan Selim was surprised at this shot, looked at Hayırbey, and Hayırbey reported to the Sultan after his brief search that all of the heavy cannons were fixed in the sand and unavailable except that single shot made by a deaf artilleryman.

In the sources of that era, the severity of the Ottoman fire power was narrated as such a big noise, everywhere was covered with a smoke and one layer of the earth erupted to the air.

To avoid the artillery and musketry, Mamluks drove the camels toward the Ottomans' ranks. Afterwards, by supporting this herd of about a thousand camels connected to each other with elephants, hiding behind them, they started to attack. Yavuz responded to this move by ordering janissaries to do rapid fire. The voice of cannons and guns shots frightened the animals who had never heard of this kind of noise before and the returning camels and elephants started to crush the Mamluk soldiers. When the camels ran away, the soldiers were shieldless.

The Ottomans as well used this tactic the Mamluks used by hiding behind the animals, but they used to resort to this tactic at the time of the defense, not at the time of the attack. Another characteristic of the Ottomans is that they familiarized the animals they would use for these kinds of tactics beforehand for the noises of cannons and guns.

The second phase of the battle continued with the fights of the cavalry on the wings. Mamluk units including Canberdi's fast cavalry picked themselves up after the unsuccessful attack with camels and headed towards the Ottomans' right wing. They attacked the janissary infantry. It was difficult for the infantrymen to fight with the mounted troops armed with spears. The fact that mounted troops came too close prevented the muskets to be filled and be made ready for the shooting. There was confluence among the janissaries and soldiers needed to retreat immediately.

Egyptian cavalry under the command of Canberdi Gazali bypassed the musketeers and reached where the Grand Vizier Sinan Pasha was located. Sinan Pasha, realizing that they were in very critical condition, rode his horse toward the hottest part of the battle immediately. He rapidly slipped into the ranks of Mamluks. Meanwhile, the distance between the right wing and the center was widened; Sinan Pasha needed reinforcements immediately but this aid was late. The grand vizier himself entered the fray and was wounded in many parts of his body by arrows and sword strikes. The upper level governors and commanders entering the battle beside him were martyred. Pasha continued his fight until he no longer could stay on horseback and when he was unable to bear anymore he was taken into a tent, severely wounded; he encouraged his soldiers for a while and even if he returned to his headquarters after witnessing that the counterattack had been successful, he fell as a martyr.

Sinan Pasha

Even though Yavuz Sultan Selim Khan, seeing that the right wing was shaken, sent cavalry soldiers immediately and the Mamluk attack was repulsed with this aid, what happened to the Grand Vizier Sinan Pasha upset everyone. However, the battle was still on and the army couldn't break down. The Ottoman army gathered again and quickly stormed the right wing, which had been under the most intensive Mamluk attack, and dispersed the Circassians there.

Sultan Selim was very upset about the martyrdom of his beloved vizier. Combining the fact that he conquered Cairo identified with Prophet Joseph, and at the same time Joseph was Sinan Pasha's first name, he said: "It is a fact that we took the throne; however, we lost Joseph."

Sinan Pasha, originally from Bosnia, was promoted from being a chief white eunuch at the palace to the Ottoman's second man, the Grand Vizier, and was a very hardworking, brave, honest, and sincere person. While many viziers, statesmen, and commanders had their share from the fury of the hardest Sultan in the Ottoman history, he never received any punishment. For days the Sultan felt grief for his grand vizier whom he loved so much and he appreciated his disciplined work. For this reason, he did not appoint anybody to the position of grand vizier for 16 days and at last he assigned Vizier Yunus Pasha to replace the martyr. This loss shaded the joy of the victory of Ridaniya; everyone was mourning, and even the Sultan joined this lamentation the very next day by wearing black clothes. His corpse was buried at the Timurtash Dervish Lodge the day following the victory, and then Sultan Selim Khan decreed that a shrine would be built over him.

The pitched battle continued at Ridaniya with intervals of seven to eight hours and finished on a Thursday, the 22nd of January, 1516. The Egyptian army was completely destroyed; the surviving Mamluk emirs as well as Tumanbay escaped around Cairo. Although the battle was over, Rumelian soldiers waited on horseback in vigilance in the battlefield that night as a precautionary measure. In addition, leading troops were dispatched around the area. After two days, the Ottoman army entered Cairo. Meanwhile, some of the Mamluk governors joined the Ottoman ranks.

The Battle of Ridaniya opened the doors of Cairo and Egypt and introduced a new continent to the Ottomans. There was a tough battle with less force fought for a longer period of time than the forces had fought in Marj Dabiq. The Sultan did not expect the Mamluks to show that much resistance. First, the Battle of Gaza and then the Pitched Battle of Ridaniya were laborious and arduous wars for which the Ottoman army fought after coming a long way. The Battle of Ridaniya shows the success of the Ottoman intelligence and the army's ability to maneuver quickly according to this intelligence.

THE SULTAN IS IN CAIRO

Sultan Selim Khan warned that the civilians wouldn't be touched during the fight against the resisting ones to restore the order in Cairo after the Battle of Ridaniya.

Yavuz Sultan Selim Khan entering Cairo

With his declarations, he guaranteed that the ones who asked for mercy wouldn't be touched.

Following the entrance and declaration of commitment of Mamluk governors, the son of Al-Ashraf Qansuh al-Ghawri, Muhammad, came into the presence of the Sultan and declared his commitment to him. He provided some of high-ranking obedient Mamluk civil servants to continue their missions.

The Sultan asked that a tent to be established outside of the city. The people of Cairo crowded around to see the Ottoman Sultan. The residents showed affection to the Sultan proceeding under the protection of 10,000 janissaries. The Sultan visited the mosques and toured the Palace of Al-Ghawri in Cairo.

While visiting, the keys of the palace were presented to him; however, Yavuz Selim Khan did not accept this offer; instead of staying in this marvelous palace, he preferred to stay in the tent again, and exiting the city, he arrived at his pavilion on the banks of the Nile River.

A rare portrait of Sultan Selim with a beard

Previously he also did not stay in Shah Ismail's magnificent Palace, Hasht-Bihisht, in the conquered city of Tabriz; instead, he was at ease in his pavilion. In a sense, the Sultan was giving a message that the real Sultanate doesn't happen by living in palaces, but only happens with modesty.

If the ratio of the time the Ottoman Sultans who spent in Edirne and Istanbul palaces during the time of their Sultanate is statistically calculated, it would be seen that Sultan Selim is one of those spending the least time in palaces.

The Sultan took in the beauty and the history of Cairo with admiration and liked the oriental aura of the city very much.

After Cairo was controlled, the town criers crying out "Aman-ı Sultan ibn Osman" (Mercy of the Sultan, son of Osman) declared that everyone was pardoned. Public life returned to normal again.

While everything seemed fine in Cairo, the first surprise the Sultan experienced was street clashes in Cairo. The Ottoman army, having had momentous victories in Marj Dabiq, Gaza, and Ridaniya, this time, was having the fourth fight with Mamluks in Cairo. The fact that Tumanbay was still alive had triggered Cairo resistance.

Tumanbay had run away somewhere around Said and sat on the edge of Nile. He was so miserable. His idea was to submit himself to Sultan Selim and be released from this miserable life; however, one of the governors opposed this again and persuaded the Mamluk ruler to do something crazy. Upon this, Tumanbay put a crazy plan into action to raid the Ottoman military camp in Cairo. He was expecting that people of Cairo and Mamluk governors would support him.

Tumanbay was going to raid Sultan's pavilion directly around sunset along with 7,000 soldiers. The Ottoman intelligence was informed about the developments immediately and the security measures at Sultan's pavilion were increased. The guards expanded the security cordon.

Ottoman soldiers shooting with a gun

The soldiers lit fires everywhere to check the surroundings. To convey the message that the raid was known and to intimidate those who would dare to raid the Ottoman military camp, they shot guns for hours.

Guns did not stop until the early morning light. This time, Tumanbay preferred to enter Cairo at Isha time. He was thinking that it would be more appropriate to head towards the Sultan's pavilion with the participation of the public once he had the control of the city.

TUMANBAY IS IN CAIRO

He got some help from the public while entering Cairo. He set up headquarters near Shayhuniya Madrasa. Not all of the Ottoman soldiers were gathered together. Some of them were staying in abandoned houses in groups of five or ten. Mamluks started to massacre Ottoman soldiers in their sleep by raiding houses one by one.

At the Ottoman military camp, the Sultan consulted with the Mamluk governors who brought intelligence about the raid and asked why Tumanbay, who fled after the war, returned suddenly, and wanted them to answer the questions. The governors said that Tumanbay was connected with some of the people of Cairo.

Mamluks entering the city continued to murder the Ottoman soldiers, whom they captured in their houses, through torture. Resources narrate that some of the Ottoman soldiers were slaughtered by sword and some of them were murdered with various torture methods such as being fixed on a skewer and being fried as kebab.

Tumanbay's men also planned to capture the Cairo castle; however, Yavuz, predicting what was going to happen in advance, left a military camp there. Ottoman soldiers started to resist the Mamluks' raid by shutting the doors. Tumanbay on the other hand formed a defense line by entering the Grand Mosque (Sultan Hasan). He had barricades set up in the neighborhoods. The number of soldiers murdered that night was over a thousand.

The Ottoman military camp did not know what was going on in the city. The military camp continued to take measures for a possible raid. In the morning, it was understood that Cairo was lost.

Yavuz, gathering the council immediately, appointed Yunus Pasha and Janissary Ayas Agha to execute the enemies in Cairo.

Yunus Pasha proceeded towards Cairo with his soldiers. Mamluks barricaded the entrance and exit of the city and poured arrows at the Ottomans. Given the large number of injured soldiers, Yunus Pasha retreated but this time attacked the barricade by bringing the cannon carriages and gunmen to the front. Although the shower of arrows continued, the barricade was destroyed after an hour. Ottoman soldiers entered the city again. This time, a chest-to-chest fight began with Mamluk soldiers. The fight went on street by street. Some of the Cairo people were throwing stones and pouring boiling water over the Ottoman soldiers. Yunus Pasha chased he Mamluks up to Kayıtbay Bridge. When the losses were more than the tolerable amount, upon the shower of arrows that began at the barricade on the bridge, he had to exit the city in the evening.

Yunus Pasha appeared before Yavuz Sultan Selim and informed him that there was tough resistance in Cairo. The Sultan asked that precautions be increased. Cannons were placed at the road junctions, and gunmen and archers were positioned there; meanwhile, distributing pardon letters again, people were asked not to join the resistance.

Tumanbay

This time, Yunus Pasha went to the city along with a large group of janissaries. The army, accompanied by the Ottoman military band passing through the streets of Cairo, came all the way to the Kayıtbay Bridge without encountering any resistance. Tumanbay expanded the established barricade. The artillery and gunfire were responded by raining arrows from the other side. The Ottoman troops started to clash on the bridge and the

barricade was passed after a chest-to-chest fight. Tumanbay retreated to the Grand Mosque and reinforced there
with his forces. Receiving the message from Yunus
Pasha, the Sultan entered Cairo at dusk. Even though
janissaries went into action again for the Sultan's sake,
they still encountered resistance on the streets. Arrows,
stones, and boiling water were thrown from the houses.
The Sultan returned to the military camp.

The next day (January 30, 1517) Yavuz Sultan Selim
Khan put his armor on headed the army personally. He
did not enter the city right away, but located soldiers at
the gates by wandering around the city and then turned
to the governors and said: "God willing, today is the day
for bringing the enemy to their knees," and he went to
the Grand Mamluk Mosque. He asked his household
troops to dismount and fight on foot along with the
janissaries. Arrows and bows in their hands, gunners at
the forefront, mounted troops started to attack. Hours of
struggle were tough enough to resemble a war. The
interesting aspect was that some of the residents were
also participating by throwing stones from their houses.
The Ottomans didn't touch the public for a long time
despite their throwing stones and boiling water. However, when they reached the end of their rope, they climbed
the high buildings and caught the people supporting the
resistance. Realizing the seriousness of the situation,
Tumanbay fled the city in disguise. Setting off by ship

near the edge of Nile, he moved away towards the direction of Said.

During the fight, an arrow had hit Yunus Pasha and he had continued to direct the operation while wounded. When the Ottoman troops had much during the street fight in Cairo, they took their revenge severely on resistance fighters. Yavuz became very angry hearing that Tumanbay fled successfully.

Resistance ended only after the Sultan's participation to the war. Returning to his pavilion Sultan Selim had had erected one white and one red flag, meaning that the city was safe. He published a declaration of amnesty again addressing the public.

The Abbasid Caliph was also in Cairo during the clashes and his presence reduced the tension between the public and the Ottomans. The sources from that era tell that Ottomans had great respect for the caliph.

CATCHING TUMANBAY

T umanbay fled from Cairo to Said, and seized the cargo ships. Meanwhile, through diplomacy, Yavuz Sultan Selim wanted to announce that the Mamluk government was removed. Talking about the victories in his conquest letter to Karaca Ahmed Pasha in Aleppo, he asked this victory to be announced. Thus, a message was given to those expecting reinforcements to arrive from Mamluks in Damascus and Aleppo.

Despite being wounded, Yunus Pasha participated the first council meeting held after the battles in Cairo. The Sultan gave assignments in this meeting. He expressed his wish to appoint Yunus Pasha to the position of Grand Viziership, which was vacant after the martyrdom of Eunuch Sinan Pasha. And with their consent, he appointed the Pasha for this position. Also that a decision was made to undertake a new task, which was to send governors called "explorers" to each side.

Canberdi Gazali, one a famous Mamluk governor, commanding the Mamluk unit in the Battle of Gaza against Sinan Pasha and leaving Tumanbay after the

Battle of Ridaniya, asked the Ottomans for forgiveness and when the letter of amnesty was sent, he was accepted to the Imperial presence to show his obedience. Yavuz Sultan Selim welcomed this Mamluk governor gladly and said that if he declared loyalty he would be treated nicely and he accepted to serve the Ottomans. While Canberdi Gazali accepted to kiss the Sultan's hand, those who came next to him weren't allowed to get close to the pavilion as a safety measure. Canberdi Gazali was appointed as governor of Sofia.

The Sultan asked Canberdi's opinions about unrest in Cairo and he said that the provocation would be eliminated only if the Sultan sat on the throne of Egypt. The Sultan would have fulfilled the advice of Canberdi.

The Ka'ba in the Ottoman Period (1879)

In the next council meeting, it was decided that another amnesty letter would be sent as well addressing Tumanbay. Previously, he sent a messenger to Sultan Selim to propose peace and declared that he would have obeyed, he would have paid tribute and the name of Sultan Selim would have been recited in sermons provided that the Ottomans would withdraw from Egypt. In his message, Tumanbay had been inviting the Ottomans to a new battle if his conditions were not accepted. The letter to Tumanbay was written by the Sultan personally.

While waiting for a response from Tumanbay, Yavuz Sultan Selim sent letters to Mecca, Medina, Yanbu, and Jiddah, declaring that Egypt's new owner is the Ottomans, and requested obedience.

The Sultan entered Cairo with a grand procession on February 15, 1517, climbed up to the Cairo Castle and sat on the throne known as Prophet Joseph's symbolically with an official ceremony. This was a sign that Egypt was firmly under the control of the Ottomans. After this ceremony there were no serious events against the Ottomans in Cairo. Canberdi was right. On the day of the ceremony, extraordinary security measures was taken in Cairo by emptying houses near the castle and positioning Ottoman soldiers in them.

The Sultan followed a fine diplomacy providing the public's commitment to the Ottomans, instead of establishing the Ottoman law system in Cairo, by restoring the duties of the *madhab qadis* (the judges of particular schools of law).

After that, the most essential subject for the Sultan was the issue of Tumanbay; important statesmen was sent to the former ruler of Egypt as messengers carrying the message that he would be pardoned. However, the incoming news made the Sultan angry because Tumanbay murdered the Ottoman messengers. In response, it was attempted to gain information through the captured Mamluk governors. The documents of this inquiry are available in the archives of the Topkapı Palace. As a result of the inquiries, it appeared that Tumanbay attempted to assassinate the Sultan.

Yavuz Sultan Selim decided to attack Tumanbay again due to the murder of his messengers and the evidence of an assassination plot. In the upcoming news, it was mentioned that Tumanbay would go to Jerusalem and Damascus and on top of that he would contact Shah Ismail.

The Sultan started the preparations for a military campaign. Two days were allowed for soldiers to be gathered. A general meeting was held and firstly soldiers were sent over to Arabian tribes.

Leading troops were sent over to Tumanbay. In addition, other forces advanced on the banks of the Nile. The Rumelian soldiers passing across the other side of the Nile were attacked by Bedouin and Circassian tribes. Even if there was confusion at the beginning, the Ottoman units collected themselves in a very short time and made the desert Arabians and Egyptian Circassians of Caucasian descent feel sorry for attacking the Ottomans.

THE CONVERSATION BETWEEN
YAVUZ AND TUMANBAY

The Sultan tracked Tumanbay city by city. Finally the news reached to pavilion that Tumanbay was captured. Tumanbay was caught on the shores of a lake. The former ruler of Egypt was brought to the Ottoman pavilion; he was respectfully given a tent and his comfort was provided. Afterwards, Yavuz and Tumanbay had long conversations. Their dialog in the sources (with simplified text) is as follows:

Yavuz: "We sent you as messengers a couple of times just to prevent the bloodshed of Muslims and we wanted the sermon and coins to be in our names. However, you killed the messengers and now there was such a result."

Tumanbay: "The messengers you sent from Damascus were respected by me; however, Emir Allan killed them and I am also not responsible for the slaughter of other messengers; if the decline of our government and the bliss and prosperity of your government had not been appreciated, this situation would not have occurred. As for the matters of Khutbah and coins, it was well known that I had already accepted these conditions. He also said: This battle was a requirement of my duty as a Sultan given me forcibly after the death of Sultan Al-Ghawri; however, how would you explain your attack with artillery and guns to a Muslim state which was the servant of Mecca and Medina with no solid justification of cruelty and sin."

Nile River and pyramids

The Sultan was silent after this speech for a while. Then, he said: "I attacked you with the permission of fatwas of the scholars because in the past when we wanted to attack the Qizilbash for the sake of Islam, Sultan Al-Ghawri provoked Dulkadirids against us, on top of that, not being content with that, he allied with the Qizilbash and came Aleppo. He tried to prevent our military campaign; he had an eye on the lands transferred to us from our ancestors. For these reasons he needed to be punished. To tell the truth, for some reasons, Circassians do not deserve the Sultanate."

Tumanbay justified these words. And he replied by pointing the former Mamluk governors, Hayırbey and Gazali, present there at that time: "O the Sultan of the Ottomans, we know that you don't have any fault but you acted with the seduction of these demons. If they had any goodness they would have shown that to their people and benefactors." (Interestingly enough, Tumanbay was right about his evaluation about Canberdi Gazali. However, Gazali would start a great rebellion during the era of Sultan Suleiman the Magnificent and would keep the state very busy.)

Then the Sultan turned to those present in the parliament and said: "It is not reasonable to touch such a brave and courageous man, do not be defective in appreciating him."

It was announced that Tumanbay was captured in Cairo. Meanwhile, operations were held concerning the public who incited riots in places. The Sultan returned to Cairo. The Sultan rested and on those days watched an interesting hunt on the Nile. Hunters were hunting a crocodile. He went to visit pyramids the next day. He admired the architecture of pyramids.

He wanted to get information about these structures. He was wondering how these pyramids were made and by whom. He asked the people around him to find a knowledgeable person. An expert on this subject could not be found. All they could get was an old man saying that he was knowledgeable. This person telling several fables about pyramids said that he did not know who constructed the pyramids and no one could understand their secret. The Sultan got information about Cairo from him.

In the meetings he held during the following days, he appointed new head governors for Egypt. Meanwhile, the issue of what was going to happen to Tumanbay was keeping the Sultan's mind busy. On the other hand, the ideas of former Mamluk governors were quite different about Tumanbay, whom the Sultan did not want to execute and appreciated the intelligence and bravery of. Hayırbey and Canberdi kept saying that Tumanbay should have been executed. The Sultan remained hesitant. He consulted this issue with his subordinates for a long time. His idea was to get a statesman with dignity such as Tumanbay under the service of the Ottoman Empire and benefit from his abilities like he did for Hayırbey and Canberdi. He treated him very well and waited for days after informing him that if he apologized and declared his commitment, he would take him to the service of the state. However, Tumanbay was telling the people around him that, aside from apologizing, he was caught in a very unfortunate way and he was about to achieve victory.

Tumanbay was executed after the consultation due to the great respect of Egyptian people, the things Tumanbay had done before, and his not attempting to apologize and enter the service of the Ottoman Empire as well as to prevent bloodshed due to any disorder against the government and religion caused by new provocations. It was announced that retribution was needed according to the religion and common law and the reason for his execution was that he caused strife among Muslims, and slaughtered the messengers and Muslim judges.

THE DEATH RISK OF THE SULTAN

Yavuz Sultan Selim did not want to stay in Cairo. One of his men that he had been expecting for a long time arrived precisely in these days. Kurdoğlu Musluhiddin Reis, sent by Oruc Reis in Algeria with the order of the Sultan, arrived in Cairo with his ships on the Nile River. The Sultan was very happy about the arrival of Kurdoğlu, one of the great Turkish sailors. He accepted him and received information about the status of the navy. Following the arrival of the Ottoman navy, he set up his pavilion on Ravza Island on the Nile. Viziers and soldiers were located on the opposite shores of the island. Sultan Selim used Kurdoğlu's ship for his round trips on the Nile.

The Sultan encountered the risk of death twice while staying on this island. The first time, Kanısev al-Adili, one of Tumanbay's governors, tried to assassinate the Ottoman Sultan. The Mamluk governor approached the island secretly where the Sultan was located along with his men; however, when he was noticed by the guards, he could barely save his own life by jumping into the river.

The second time the Sultan encountered the risk of death was as a result of an accident. The Sultan's feet slipped when he tried to get on the dock from the boat due to the slippery wood. When Yavuz fell into the Nile, an Egyptian who was a good swimmer immediately rushed to help the Sultan and saved him.

The ships coming from Istanbul with full of provisions could only have reached Alexandria in three months unfortunately due to storms. The Sultan as well went to Alexandria to see and inspect the navy personally. After seeing the navy ships he also took a walk around Alexandria. This city was the second largest city and the most important port in Egypt. It was a historical city with its foundation dating back to Alexander of Macedon.

The Sultan came to Alexandria on a Friday. He not only performed the Friday Prayer in the mosque of Garbi, but he also visited the office of our Prophet, peace and blessing be upon him, the place that was believed to have the footprint of Ali, Masjid ar-Rahma where Amr ibn As sat when he entered the city second time, the Mosque of Abu al-Abbas known as the office of Abu al-Abbas and Yakut Shazali. After the *Asr* Prayer, he left the city and moved towards Cairo.

After coming to Cairo, he sent messengers to the island of Cyprus, who had paid annual taxes to the Mamluks, and said that the taxes would be paid to the Ottomans now.

Some measures were taken for the procession going on a pilgrimage from Egypt. This was the first pilgrimage convoy leaving Egypt under Ottoman domination. Yavuz developed the tradition of sending money for the services and officials in the holy lands, which the Ottomans had been performing since the age of Sultan Bayezid I or even further. During this period, the Sultan sent money to Mecca and Medina from both Istanbul and Cairo. He increased the amount of money he sent to several times more than the amount of money his father sent. The money was distributed to those in the registry by an official under the supervision of two *qadis* and people getting the money finished a complete reading of the Qur'an along with the prayers afterwards for the Sultan.

Thirty memorizers of the Qur'an were designated, and each of them was asked to recite one chapter of the Qur'an every day and by doing so, a complete reading of the Qur'an everyday was completed. It was decided that these hafizes were given twelve gold coins annually. Afterwards, the poor in these holy lands were called, their names were registered in the notebook and each member of the family was provided with three gold coins every year. In addition, in the memoirs of the Lieutenant General Ibrahim Rifat Pasha, it was documented that Yavuz Sultan Selim was the first person organizing "grain charity" for the people of Mecca and Medina. The grains were distributed to the public, the leftovers were sold, and the earnings were also given to the public.

Again, an official sent during Yavuz's era gathered the poor at the square, gave each one of them one gold coin and asked them to perform Umra on behalf of the mother of the Sultan, Ayşe Hatun, and then these people performed Umra for deceased Sultana by wearing the special pilgrimage garment.

Surra means money pouch and it the materialization of the Ottoman's love and responsibility for Mecca and Medina. Through Surra, a variety of dressings, sanjaks, and serious amount of money was sent. This money was distributed to the officials as well as the poor of Mecca and Medina and used for the facilities such as water channels, hospitals, and outposts to make the duties of Haj and Umra easy.

The first Surra was sent from Edirne during the era of Yıldırım Bayezid and this tradition was continued by other Sultans, and since the era of Fatih Sultan Mehmed, it was sent from Istanbul. Since the Surra sent from Istanbul reached Mecca and Medina through Damascus, it used to be called Surra of Damascus or Mahmil of Damascus.

The Ottoman Surras changed into completely different shapes beginning the era of Yavuz Sultan Selim; not only were they now more magnificent but also two Surras were sent from the country of the Ottomans, one from Istanbul and another from Cairo.

Meanwhile, the preparations to return to Istanbul began. Four thousand janissaries would have been sent to the port of Beirut and the Navy would have spent the winter on the island of Cyprus. The booty would be taken to Alexandria through the land and they would be transferred to the ships from there.

After a couple of days, the son of Mecca Sheriff, the descendant of our Prophet, came to Cairo. Sultan Selim showed him great respect and had him sit next to the Grand Vizier. The son of the sheriff came to submit his obedience for the Ottoman Empire and to talk about how the following administration would be. The Sultan declared that Mecca and Medina are holy places and they would be administered autonomously by sheriffs as in their former status.

In the letter written by Selman Reis who was sent by Yavuz Sultan Selim to protect the holy places from Portuguese occupation, it was told that the Portuguese ships were sent away from the vicinity of Jeddah and the sheriff of Mecca supported them. The Sultan was very happy about this letter. The sheriff of Mecca by himself was already not pleased with the Mamluk administration, which could not have protected the holy lands against the Christian threat.

The son of the sheriff of Mecca, Abu Numay, presented the gifts to show a commitment to the Sultan on behalf of his father. Among the gifts, most of which have been preserved until today in the Office of Holy Relics in the Topkapı Palace, there were the keys of the Ka'ba and Prophet Muhammad's Cardigan (the Cardigan of

Happiness). Abu Numay got dressed in the robe of honor and he was sent away with a warrant showing that his father was granted as an emirate and a robe of honor for his father.

Two hundred thousand gold coins and plenty of rations were sent to be distributed among the people of Mecca and Medina; moreover, some of the notables of Mecca imprisoned in Cairo during the time of Al-Ghawri were released. Thus, not only were Mecca and Medina taken under the Ottoman patronage but also, as a sign of this, the Ottoman Sultans would have been called by the title of "the servant of glorious Mecca and Medina." This address consists of a great Ottoman humility in itself. The title Mamluks used to use was "the protector of glorious Mecca and Medina," which carried a little bit of pride.

Evliya Çelebi describes this incident in a very nice way: When the Sultan was called "the ruler of Mecca and Medina" in the sermon during the Friday Prayer performed after 1517 Ridaniya Victory, the Sultan interfered and corrected as "the servant of Mecca and Medina" and he could not help himself crying after the change in the sermon. Following the Prayer, the Sultan presented a variety of generous gifts and compliments to the preacher. The Ottomans used the title of "the servant of Mecca and Medina" in official documents, printed on gold money and preached in sermons. Caliph Abdulmecid Effendi was the last person using this title used from the time of Yavuz. After the abolition of the caliphate, this title has been used by the kings of Saudi Arabia.

Meanwhile, some of the Mamluk notables including Caliph Mutevekkil and his uncle Halil's sons as well as Al-Ghawri's son Muhammad, scholars and artisans, architects, building masters, and some traders were sent to Istanbul. The intention of the Sultan was to show that the center of the caliphate was not Cairo anymore, but Istanbul.

The reason the Sultan stayed in the region for about eight months was to establish a permanent system in Egypt. Because of the public safety, strengthening the Ottoman domination in these regions and having them enter the Ottoman's administration especially when the Portuguese threat over the Red Sea was causing serious trouble was making it mandatory to take new military measures. That the Sultan was personally taking care of the business provided the system to be settled more robustly.

Soldiers and statesmen was complaining that they had stayed in Egypt for too long; moreover, soldiers could not collect fees due to being far away from their land and for this reason they had financial difficulties. The presentation of this topic to the Sultan required great courage. Those who knew what happened before, and knew of the Sultan's temper, could not find the courage to mention the return. For this reason chief military judge Kemalpashazade, who the Sultan respected, was made to be the messenger. The chief military judge knew the Sultan's rage very well. At an appropriate time he mentioned that soldiers were homesick so much so that they make a song. When the Sultan asked what the song was, he replied:

> What we have left in the land of Arabia
> Why do we still stay in Damascus and Aleppo?
> People of the world are entertaining themselves
> Let's go to the Rumelia.

The Sultan liked these lyrics very much and accelerated the preparations by saying "from now on, we don't have anything for us to stay here, let's go back." Then in the following chat, he asked Kemalpashazade about Molla Lutfi. He implied that he made up this stanza like Lutfi, who had troubles due to his fabricated skits. The chief military greeted the Sultan by saying "the Sultan's intuition is the most accurate witness." The Sultan as well kept his silence even though he understood that the song was a fabrication; it seemed like he was satisfied with the presentation of a legitimate request in a nice way, then he sent 500 golden coins for Kemalpashazade.

RETURN TO ANATOLIA

Yavuz Sultan Selim, assigning the administration of Egypt to Hayırbey and giving him some recommendations, confirmed the order to leave the city after selecting which soldiers would stay and dividing the rest into five groups. The Sultan set off from Cairo and reached Gaza. He arrived at Damascus after a long walk. Winter would be spent in Damascus. The month of Ramadan started. The Sultan and his soldiers performed their fast in Damascus.

When the *Eid al-Fitr* (Ramadan feast) came, the Sultan again exchanged *bayram* (festival) greetings with the statesmen and commanders in his pavilion and then he went to the Umayyad Mosque for the *Eid* Prayer.

Those who wanted to see the Sultan at the mosque were very surprised. He came wearing a simple black outfit without any indicated that he was the Sultan. The simplicity-loving Sultan was showing everybody that there should not be pretension in the mosque.

After Yavuz Sultan Selim performed the *Eid* Prayer, he visited the newly built tomb of Sheikh Muhyiddin ibn Arabi and he ordered a mosque and complex of buildings to be built adjacent to the tomb.

According to intelligence about the activities of Shah Ismail, various measures were taken. Afterwards, spies informed him that the Shah, who had learned that the Sultan was in Damascus, withdrew.

The death of his teacher whom he loved so much and constantly kept near to himself, Halimi Effendi, shook the Sultan deeply. He performed the Funeral Prayer, and a cloud of grief wrapped the whole city, and stores were shut down. The Sultan had his teacher buried near the tomb of Muhyiddin ibn Arabi.

Wearing mourning clothes, Yavuz Sultan Selim withdrew into himself after the death. He did not attend the council meetings. He did not eat and drink properly. He retreated into a corner for days and spent his time with only prayers and supplications. He ended his retreat due to the recent news coming from the East.

His days were spent with new appointments and military precautions. The Sultan reached another Eid in Damascus and performed the *Eid-al-Adha* in the Umayyad Mosque. Meanwhile, he was very happy about the news that Egyptian pilgrims reached Mecca safely. Since this was the first pilgrimage done under the Ottoman administration, he took this matter that the pilgrims would go to the holy lands safely seriously.

Due to the soldiers' inability to collect fees because of the long military campaigns, the Sultan relieved them by lending money to the needy from the treasury. These financial books, kept by the Ottomans who respected records very much, survived until today after five centuries. They are stored in the Ottoman archives of the premiership.

After settling the matter of Ibn Hanash, who was being a bandit on the roads, the Sultan made Piri Pasha who came from Istanbul to Damascus, the Grand Vizier. The Sultan performed the Friday Prayer again in the Umayyad mosque.

The following week was the time for loyalty for Muhyiddin ibn Arabi who informed that he would come centuries ago. The Sultan performed the following Friday Prayer in the mosque built next to the tomb of Muhyiddin ibn Arabi. Yavuz was the first Sultan performing the first Friday Prayer in this new mosque. He had built a mosque and a dervish lodge on the tomb and public soup kitchen across from that. Over time, when these works of art eroded, Sultan Abdulhamid Khan repaired them and allowed them to survive to the present day.

On his way back from Damascus, after participating in the hunt near Aleppo, the Sultan went to Antioch from there. He visited the mosque of Habib al-Najjar (Habib the Carpenter).

By giving notice to Anatolia, he ordered that bows and arrows be prepared to provide for the army. By staying in the region, the Sultan wanted to meet Shah Ismail one last time. However, after changing his mind, he returned to Istanbul but left Piri Pasha in the region.

While the exact cause for this change of mind was not known, the Sultan probably wanted to return to Istanbul and aimed to head towards the East again depending on the course of the events on the West border. Leaving Piri Pasha there was a sign of his intention to return.

The Sultan, coming to Istanbul from Kayseri, Aksaray, and Afyon, lingered when he heard that there were festivities organized in Istanbul to meet him. He came by ship and entered the Topkapı Palace secretly on the 25th of July, 1518, at the time of Isha Prayer. It took two years for the Sultan to leave the palace and return again.

Yavuz Sultan Selim

LAST YEARS

When informed about the new political developments of crusader alliance in the West, the Sultan stayed in Istanbul for only 10 days and went
to Edirne afterwards. Yavuz Sultan Selim already preferred to spend most of his time in Edirne rather than
Istanbul.

While the Sultan was in Edirne, Shah Veli, the son
of Shah Celal, revolted in Sızır, a town connected to
Gemerek, the district of Sivas in the region of Sivas-
Bozok (Yozgat). Shah Ismail's supporters were gathering
around this man.

According to the sources of that era, Shah Veli
resided in a big and deep cave around Turhal Castle
and was successful in tricking the local people, the
majority of which were Rafizids of Ismailiyye and pro-
fane and idle people, who started to come to his side.
While previously mentioning the reason he preferred
to stay in that area because it was a place for Saints,
after the number of his visitors increased, he started to
say bizarre remarks such that they did not choose that

place by themselves but the wandering dervishes made a commitment that Mahdi would appear in the cave soon. He even gave fatwas that removed all of the Islamic prohibitions. Shah Veli was saying that he learned this way from Mahdi. He introduced himself to a large number of people who pledged alliance to him as the supporter of Mahdi. His so-called disciples exaggerated so much so that they started to bow and prostrate to him. New and great strife emerged in Anatolia. Sources narrate that in twelve days, 50,000 people including women, men, and children became subjects of Shah Veli.

Shah Ismail played a role in the emergence of this strife personally. The rebel named Celal from now on would give his name to other rioters causing trouble in Anatolia and every rebel would be called "Celali." By saying: "Arrows don't sting me and swords don't cut me," and attacking the towns and villages of Yozgat, Celal launched the rebellion.

When caught, one of his disciples mentioned that Shah Veli was connected with Shah Ismail. Shah Veli was trying to spread from Middle and Eastern Black Sea region to the area of Sivas-Adana.

Shah Veli became aggressive when the number of his so-called disciples reached a certain level. Accompanied by 4,000 people, he first ransacked the house of the son of Şehsuvaroğlu Ali Bey. When Amasya governor general Sadi Pasha, fighting against rebels, went to

Zile to collect soldiers to fight, he was attacked by Shah Veli and ignoring the small number of soldiers he had, he had entered into battle. However, he lost a great deal and was only able to retreat to Amasya wounded and with difficulty. Then, gathering his strength, he attacked Shah Veli one more time; however, he couldn't do anything due to the crowd accumulated around Shah Veli.

When this news reached Sultan Selim, he sent repeated orders for necessary measures to be taken and these orders immediately were applied knowing that, if not, people would be punished severely. He dispatched Ferhad Pasha, whom he appointed as a vizier to that region. Two of the Ottoman pashas, the governor Hüsrev and Shadi Pasha, were on the move as well.

By joining their forces, Hüsrev Pasha and Şehsuvaroğlu Ali Bey started to follow rebels on the 23rd of April, 1519. Ferhad Pasha was around Ankara at that time. Upset due to the movements of the Ottoman troops in the region, the rebels retreated. Upon the retreat of Bozoklu Celal, Şehsuvaroğlu Ali Bey, and the governors of Karaman and Rumelia seized this opportunity and without waiting for the arrival of Ferhad Pasha, they went after the rebels. The Ottoman army caught up the Bozoklu's forces and started to fight with them.

The troops of the Ottoman Empire, the most powerful army in the 16th century, defeated the rebels quickly and punished them severely.

Shah Veli and the people close to him managed to escape. But they were not alone. Uveys, Şehsuvaroğlu Ali's son, followed them and met a group of people who caught Bozoklu Celal and one of his close men upon an order they had received. By taking Shah Veli from their hands, he sent him to his father accompanied by a knowledgeable person. Shadi Pasha reported this adventure to the Sultan in detail. Shadi Pasha wrote that he assumed that he would be transported to the Sultan's presence alive. However, Şehsuvaroğlu did not send him alive. Sources from that era tell that Şehsuvaroğlu Ali Bey acted that way because he wanted to show everybody if arrows really sting and swords really cut him. It was appropriate to show everybody what he was telling was not right to prevent a fake Sheikh or Saint to start more strife.

When the rebellion was finished, a rumor erupted about Shahzadah Murad, son of Shahzadah Ahmed, who was reportedly alive and about to reach Anatolia. The Sultan was furious and appointed people to investigate this issue. As a result of the investigations, it was understood that the news was untrue.

During the time he stayed in Edirne, the Sultan revised his relations with European governments and he followed up on the activities of crusaders under the leadership of Pope making the preparations to attack the Islamic world.

The Pope had tried to prevent Yavuz to negotiate with the Hungarians, had provoked the Knights of Rhodes, and had convinced France to be the pioneer for a new crusade. The belief that the Ottoman Empire was the biggest enemy of Christianity had been around since the establishment of this Grand State and would not change until the final fall.

The Pope's dreams of tearing the Ottoman Empire down continued constantly. Finally, the Pope called for a decision at the Lateran council about whether a crusade should be held. He ordered experienced commanders to make plans for war against Yavuz Sultan Selim. He prepared six questions and wanted answers:

1. Is a battle necessary?

2. If yes, should that be an offensive or defensive battle?

3. What are the possible issues preventing the battle and how could they be removed?

4. Do all of the rulers or some of them engage the battle; who would those be?

5. Which of the facilities should help the battle be carried out?

6. How the battle should be actualized?

The answers to these questions would be beneficial to determine the strategy of the battle and the military campaign; however, everything was coming down to money.

In the prospective military campaign, the number of the soldiers included 60,000 infantry, 12,000 light cavalry, and 4,000 dragoons. For the navy, Venice, Genoa, Naples, Spain, and Portugal could contribute. While the Pope sent detailed reports to the emperor and the king of France, his surrogates sent them to other rulers.

I. François responded positively (23 September 1517). The Emperor as well prepared his answers; however, this response reached Rome only in February of 1518. The received responses in fact were reflecting the jealousy of the two great rulers against each other; however, with the positive responses he got from other rulers, the Pope announced this joyous situation the 14th of March, 1518, by organizing a ritual in the Church of Maria Minevra. Apparently, everything was planned and thought out in depth. However, various problems prevented the Pope from organizing the military campaign.

The death of the Emperor Maximilian on the 12th of January, 1519 and the starting Imperial struggle changed the situation in Europe completely. And the idea of the crusade could not proceed further than just being a dream. According to the Venetian ambassador Contarini's report written on the 3rd of April, 1519, even Spaniards sent an ambassador to the Sultan and searched for a deal. The ambassador declared that they were expecting exemptions the Mamluk Sultans had accepted for the Camame Church and Christian Monks to be continued. The Sultan greeted this ambassador very well and accepted him as interlocutor. However, for these requests to be accepted, he asked that another ambassador whom the Spanish king personally gave complete authority, along with a letter, be sent. The treaty with the Hungarians had been extended. The Sultan accepted the Venetian ambassador who brought the money for Cyprus and addressed the ambassador unusually while he was leaving: "As long as the Venetian government obeys the provisions of the last treaty word for word, the state of peace would continue." The Venetian government, which could not take the chance to fight against a state with such a powerful Sultan, complied with the requests.

The Sultan went on a hunting expedition around Komotini in the winter of 1518, and received news when he was at the site of Karasu Yenicesi. He received intelligence that some of the Christian ships would loot the coasts of Thrace. Sultan Selim investigated the situation and immediately learned that these ships were waiting near the island of Thassos. All the Christian ships' plans to ambush were ruined by two Ottoman boats. Thinking that an Ottoman fleet was following these boats, the Christians left the ships and scattered around the island. When this situation was conveyed to the Sultan, soldiers were transferred to the island immediately. Due to severe winter conditions, those who took refuge on the island were in a difficult situation and about 70–80 of them were caught and sent to the Sultan. Probably these were the Christian pirate ships circulating in the Aegean Sea and operating related to Rhodes.

When returning from Edirne to Istanbul, the first thing Sultan Selim Khan did was to order the preparation of the army. Meanwhile, he had a marble mansion made on the edge of the sea. The ships were being built, cannons were being prepared, and oarsmen were being collected.

All summer was spent with the preparations of the navy and related work. The Sultan, who had stayed in Trabzon as a shahzadah for years, knew about marine issues and ships.

All of these preparations had one goal: Rhodes. After Egypt and Syria became Ottoman residences, with this Christian outpost preventing Istanbul's connection with sea removed, the security of the Mediterranean would be resolved. However, an incident erupted while talking about Rhodes, and turned the agenda upside down. A riot supporting Safavids started in Anatolia. In addition to that, the unsuitable weather conditions caused the Rhodes military campaign to be postponed to the following year.

The Sultan himself did not have a positive outlook on a military campaign to Rhodes. The Sultan, seeing that his viziers next to him were very enthusiastic about the conquest of the island, said: "You want to take me to the infidels' island. Is that worth it for me to go there? It would be hard to conquer. It is not even certain how we will conquer with prepared viziers such as yourselves. How would you conquer it without making the necessary preparations? Does the honor of the reign carry this, if it fails? To conquer a mere castle means a great deal of difficulty and heaps of trouble. The most important need to conquer a castle is gunpowder. How long will your rations and gunpowder last? Answer me!"

While viziers informed him that rations and other tools were ready, they could not say anything for the gunpowder since they did not have any knowledge of this question. The next day, viziers said that gunpowder had been accumulated for four-and-a-half or five months and it was enough to meet their needs. Upon hearing this, the Sultan looked at his men with furrowed brows and said: "Now, not only in five months, but even in six months, you can't conquer that place. Not even in seven months. God knows, it may only be conquered in eight or nine months. It is not possible with these supplies. As long as it's not for the Hereafter, I don't set out for a military campaign." With these words, it seemed like the Sultan was relating how long it would take to get Rhodes in the time of Suleiman the Magnificent and the words he expressed in the end was indicated his preparations for the Hereafter.

The conquest of Rhodes, which was surrounded but not conquered by his grandfather, Sultan Mehmed the Conqueror, would be granted to Suleiman the Magnificent and the conquest of the castle would take nine months.

The Castle of Seven Towers, where the surplus of the treasure kept during the period of Sultan Selim

THE LAST TRAVEL TO
THE ETERNAL REALM

The military campaign towards Rhodes was post-poned. The Sultan was planning to go to Edirne. In the garden of Topkapı Palace, while going for a walk with the father of the historian Hodja Sadeddin Effendi, he complained about a pain on his back and said that he was feeling a tingle like the prick of a thorn.

Hasan Can said that it was not serious. It could be a splinter or a thorn and if the Sultan permitted, he could have a look. When he examined his back he saw acne with whitened tip. When he mentioned about the acne, the Sultan wanted him to squeeze and puncture it imme-diately; however, after Hasan Can said that this could be dangerous and they need to wait by applying ointment, the Sultan replied: "I am not a boy, so why should I con-tact a surgeon for a simple acne?" When Hasan Can did not squeeze the acne, he went to the Turkish bath the next day and had the acne to be squeezed by the bath attendant. However, the Sultan was not relieved but instead started to feel the pain more intensely. Most prob-ably the detonated acne was not a fistula, but a tumor.

There was a plague epidemic in Istanbul and the symptoms were showing that the Sultan had caught the plague. The thing appeared on his back was not a fistula, but a tumor. It grew gradually along the way and made the Sultan of the world miserable. The Sultan was in such pain that he could not stand on horseback and he was taken in a cart. The efforts of the doctors brought to him from Istanbul did not work.

The miniature showing Sultan Selim on his deathbed

The Sultan, coming up to the village of Sırt near Çorlu, was in such a dire situation that he could not walk. They had to stay there. The wound on his back in the village of Sırt knocked down the Sultan, whom no one had been able to bring down so far.

The sick Sultan participated in the council meeting in pain and he carried out the appointments and promotions. To avoid rumors among soldiers, he showed himself by standing out in front of the pavilion. At the last council he attended, he spoke of his last will about the Ottoman people and the Ottoman land. He had a secret meeting with Piri Pasha related to some important issues.

Despite the intervention of the physicians, the Sultan, whose sickness was getting worse, could not attend the council anymore. Although intensive care was given to him for about a month, it did not work and he surrendered his soul on the night connecting the 21st of September to the 22nd of September towards the morning (1520). During the moment of death, Hasan Can was attending to him. He had his last conversation with him:

"What's going on, Hasan Can?"

"Your Highness! It's time to turn to God and spend time with Him."

"What do you think we were with all this time? Did you see a flaw in our turning to God?"

"God forbid! I did not see you to be heedless even for a moment. However, this time it is not the same so I said this just for precaution."

Pausing for a moment, the Sultan then said: "Hasan Can, recite the chapter Ya-Sin."

Upon this, Hasan Can completed one recitation of the chapter Ya-Sin. He started to recite it once more.

Hasan Can saw that the Sultan was also repeating the Surah along with him. He narrated what happened at that moment to his son in the following years as: "When he came to the verse of '*Salamun qawlan mir-Rabbin Rahim*' ("Peace!" is the word from the Lord All-Compassionate) for the second time, I saw that his lips were moving as if he was repeating the mentioned verse. I raised his index finger, squeezed the rest of his fingers as a fist, held his hand, pushed his sleeves back and took his pulse.

The Chief Physician Ahi Çelebi was looking at what I was doing. When he saw my efforts he scolded me: "He is still alive, why are you acting strangely?" Then I said: "Since I started serving at this door, I did not turn my face away even for a moment from the service to my benefactor. At this moment he needs this, there is no need for a physician, our precious is gone."

Hasan Can tried hard to hide the death of the Sultan. This news could cause great turmoil in the army outside of the city.

That morning the council was held as usual, but the situation of the Sultan was not disclosed. The usual necessities were performed. Seemingly, everything was going on as normal. In the meantime, the physicians, Shah Kazvini, doctor Isa and doctor Osman took care of the body and enshrouded him. Hasan Can reported that while being washed, the Sultan covered his private parts twice with his right hand and the washers expressed their awe by exaltation of God and salutes to the Prophet. A notice was sent to Manisa to inform the only heir of the throne, Shahzadah Suleiman, and the news that Yavuz left this world would be kept as a secret until he came to Istanbul.

After the Shahzadah came to Istanbul and ascended the throne, Piri Pasha gathered the commanders and deputies and said: "Comrades! This is the ordinance and God's will. His Majesty Yavuz Sultan Selim Khan transcended to the Hereafter. Our Sultan, His Majesty, ascended the throne in Istanbul with happiness and prosperity, go and be there." Suddenly, commanders felt great sorrow. Some slammed their heads onto the ground. Some slapped the ground. When the news spread through the army, a deep silence fell. Sobs were the only thing breaking the silence. The sturdy Sultan, commanding the loyal soldiers, passed away. The return to Istanbul began. The army flowed into the capital like a silent river.

The Sultan's funeral was greeted by a large crowd in Edirnekapı. Sultan Suleiman came under his father's coffin, carried that for a while, and then viziers came under the coffin. The coffin was brought up to Fatih Mosque on their shoulders. The great scholar of that era, Zembilli Ali Effendi, led the Funeral Prayer of the exceptional Sultan of the Ottoman Empire. Then he was transferred to where today's tomb is located. A tent was set up on his grave and a tomb in his name was founded by his son. The yet uncompleted mosque was finished.

ALL THAT WAS LEFT FROM A SULTAN

Yavuz Sultan Selim Han, regarded as the Conqueror of the East, was the first Sultan to consider the prevention of the Safavid threat as the most important mission. His struggle with Iran in this period provided the Ottoman religious understanding from the Sunni point of view.

The Sultan aimed to gather the Islamic world under one flag and brought the servitude of Mecca and Medina to the Ottomans. To dominate all of the Red Sea for the protection of the holy land was one of his ideas as well. During his period, the Ottomans went to a new continent, Africa, for the first time.

While the meaning of his nickname, Yavuz, is naughty or tough, after it has been used with Sultan Selim, its meaning changed and transformed into keen, hardcore, or unbending.

Physically, he was described as being of medium height close to being tall, frowning and hard-eyed, beardless, had a long bush beard, round-faced and Roman-nosed. Drawings of him with an earring have nothing to do with reality. The miniatures drawn in his era show no earring on the Sultan's ears, and the sources of that era do not mention such a habit of the Sultan.

This painting presumed to be the drawing of Yavuz Sultan Selim has nothing to do with the Sultan. (Ottoman Sultans don't wear an earring, necklace, or a crown above turban).

Sultan Selim, who is a leader with the characteristics of devoting himself to state affairs, didn't like entertainment and the life of harem. His only pleasure was to go hunting and doing arms drills. He used all the weapons of his era such as sword, arrow, gun and so on very well.

STATESMANSHIP

One of the most important reasons for his success in state affairs is to follow the orders he gave strictly. The Sultan, who was restless in the realization of the work he decided to do, never blinked before removing the obstacles interfering with the work to be done. If necessary he didn't hesitate to apply the most severe penalties as well. When he promised things, he kept his promise. It is known that besides with his toughness he also had a gentle nature and refined speech. He didn't like pretension, flamboyance, and gimmickry at all. He warned Shahzadah Suleiman on this issue.

Viziers were the most affected by the fury of the Sultan who got angry when there was looseness, incompetence, or delays in fulfilling decisions taken and due to this, in the following years among viziers the biggest and famous curse was to say: "I wish you would be the vizier of the Sultan." However, a point on the other hand to know is the meticulousness of the Sultan in the selection of his men. Sometimes he even didn't appoint any vizier and he sometimes kept the position of the Grand Vizier vacant. According to rumors, Sultan Murad IV ascending to the throne centuries later than Sultan Selim, taking an example by his great grandfather Yavuz, girded himself with a sword of our Prophet, peace and blessing be upon him, after Yavuz Sultan Selim's sword at the ceremony of sword at Eyub Sultan would pour out his troubles by saying: "I wish one of Sultan Selim Han's men would be present at this time."

The Sultan's stern temper is very famous. But on the other hand, sometimes there happened to be people who were exposed to his harsh words but insisted that they were correct. The Sultan appreciated those kinds of people. In this regard, the best example was the communication between him and Zembilli Ali Effendi. The Sultan ordered that the officials of treasury be executed immediately due to not fulfilling the requirements of their duties. Learning of the situation, Mufti Zembilli Ali Effendi went to the Sultan immediately and asked for mercy for the officials. Yavuz was furious. He said to Zembilli acrimoniously that this issue is a state matter and he cannot interfere with it. Upon this, by saying, "My sermon is not against the order of the Sultanate but your command is against your Hereafter. It is the a requirement of my responsibility and duty to tell you this," the famous scholar told that his real concern is the hereafter of the Sultan and his heart didn't permit him to let his Sultan to go to the afterlife with such a sin, and it was his responsibility to tell this to the Sultan as the Mufti. While everybody was expecting that the Sultan would be more furious, the Sultan softened and acknowledged that his teacher was right. With the request of Zembilli, he reappointed the officials to their jobs.

He was famous to treat his subjects with justice regardless of their religion. In 1490, it was asked that the Pammakaristos Church (Fethiye Mosque) to be converted to a mosque since it didn't have any congregation left. This topic led to a big discussion in Istanbul. This issue was transferred to the Yavuz's period. The Sultan was in struggle with Safavids and the religious sensitivity increased in the government and public. Patriarch Theoleptus I demanded justice by showing the warrant protecting the churches during the reign of Sultan Mehmed II. However, the warrant couldn't be found, since it had been burned. Upon this, the testimonies of the three surviving janissaries who witnessed the conquest of Istanbul were requested. Thereupon, Sultan Selim made a new warrant confirming the rights of Christians to the Patriarch. When this issue reenters the agenda during the reign of Kanuni, the Patriarch of that period shows that warrant from the Sultan.

In Egyptian sources, it is attention-grabbing that he is identified as a modern "Baybars" (famous Mamluk ruler) reviving a fair system. In his personality, it was assumed that the old Mamluk power was revived.

His Commandership

Yavuz Sultan Selim was a very capable military commander. He wanted his army to be kept ready all the time; he founded a very strong army with the skills of his selected commanders.

In the Ottoman history, he is one of the most dominant commanders. He never let the soldiers be involved in the matters other than their own duties. That in the first years of his Sultanate he took revenge for the riots that occurred during and on the return of the Iran expedition showed that he is dead serious.

His army was the most successful and experienced of that period. His army was unrivaled both physically and for using horses and firearms in the battlefield successfully. How the guns could be used successfully in a pitched battle was seen with him for the first time.

The Sultan, whose rules were based on the religious orders, never made a concession to violate religious orders during and on the return of an expedition. On the return of the Battle of Chaldiran, food shortages arose and then news that a small number of soldiers attacked and looted the nearby villages reached the Sultan. Not to be the commander of an army getting things illegally, to provide the discipline and to prevent the disorder, he found and executed a few of soldiers who were involved in these acts. In addition, he dismissed the Grand Vizier Ahmed Pasha and Second Vizier Dukakinoğlu Ahmed Pasha, whom he held responsible for this incident by demolishing their tents on their heads. The Sultan expressed his anger by telling them that they acted imprudently, they showed flaws in restraining the military as well as this incident occurred due to their stupidity.

"Why are you so imprudent in the precaution and not restraining them? Your lack of comprehension and shortage in mind caused this abominable situation."

Yavuz Sultan Selim Khan never experienced a defeat in any of the wars he did during his reign. Interestingly, he was defeated only once against the Ottoman forces when he was a Shahzadah fighting against his father. Even in the Egyptian sources, the Sultan, with his heroism and justice, is likened to Macedonian Alexander the Great and Sasanid ruler Anushirvan who is famous for his justice.

His Interest in the Navy

The Sultan learned seamanship very well in Trabzon, unlike of all Shahzadahs coming before him, and in his era had an immense knowledge of the navy and ships. For this reason, he gave much importance to the sea and wanted to strengthen the navy he inherited from his father.

The Sultan's preparations for the navy are described carefully in the sources of that era and in the reports of the ambassadors. The importance given to marine affairs by the Sultan is narrated by Lutfi Pasha in another imaginary anecdote as well:

"One day the late Sultan said to Kemalpashazade the deceased: I want to have 300 shipyards made, which has to be from Galata Fortress to Kağıthane, and my intention is to conquer Efrench. Molla replied: My Majesty! You reside in such a city that has the benefit of being near the sea. If the sea was not safe, ships wouldn't come and if ships wouldn't come, Istanbul would not be prosperous."

Lutfi Pasha adds that this matter was not granted to Yavuz Sultan Selim but it came true during the reign of Kanuni. This situation shows that Sultan Selim I placed importance on the construction of shipyard and establishment of the navy. By citing the conversation between the Sultan and Piri Pasha, the historian Celalzade revealed the importance given to the army by the Sultan:

"One day, when the Sultan was in Istanbul, Piri Pasha entered the council meeting and they had a meeting. By addressing the Pasha, the Sultan asked his opinion: There are lands in infidels' country with magnificent cities, steadfast ramparts and bastions, giant castles and full-fledged islands; their Sultans are all infidels; these infidels are not worthy for these lands but they rule the world; I am planning to sort out this matter." Piri Pasha understood why the Sultan started this topic and answered: "O my Sultan, let 500–600 ships be constructed on your order." The Sultan was satisfied with this and replied back: "So ordered, do it immediately." Upon this, messengers were sent everywhere to collect the materials to construct a ship. The place where shipyards were located was a complete cemetery at that time.

The work began immediately, on the same day. The corpses were transferred to another location and the bones were stacked and buried in a ditch. The boatyard was cleaned thoroughly. Three months passed and the men of Venetian governors came and brought a letter. When this news arrived to the land of infidels, they said that Sultan Selim Khan conquered the Persian and Arabian countries. Now it is our country's turn to come. We are not strong enough to encounter and to fight with him.

To be subjected to him as a requisite, eight European rulers got together and sent messengers with presents and a three-year of tribute from each one of them.

Other than that, Mustafa Ali from Gallipoli states that the construction of shipyard sections and numerous cellars for the maintenance of ships coming from sea voyage started and then completed during the reign of Suleiman the Magnificent. Shipyard sections were constructed similar to the European ones. However, its completion with the ability to hold as many as 200 ships was succeeded during the reign of Sultan Suleiman.

His Curiosity about Books

Among Ottoman Sultans, he is one of those with highest intellectual levels. The Sultan who loved to chat with scholars and poets had a principle to get the ideas of scholars and other statesmen before deciding on some of the political issues. Sultan Selim, who was very fond of reading, finished reading all of the books in his library, lived in deep contemplation until late at night and had very little sleep. He was especially interested in the libraries wherever he went. He particularly had a great curiosity about history books.

When he was in Egypt, he had the history book, *Nujumu'z-Zahira*, written by Ibn Tagrıbirdi and translated by Kemalpashazade. Among history books, he read mostly about *Tarih-i Vassaf* (The History of Vassaf). One of the most nerve-wracking issues about the books for the Sultan was the missing books.

There was a famous event during the Egypt expedition. There were desert Arabs on the way. These people didn't have the courage to attack the Ottoman army but they assailed the loads coming from behind and stole goods and animals. During one night walk, a load consisting of the Sultan's clothing was left behind and plundered by desert Arabs. In that load, there were chests of the Sultan's books and one of those chests consisted of his favorite book, *Tarih-i Vassaf*, written in beautiful calligraphy.

The Sultan was very sad about theft of the book. Upon learning this, the Sultan's teacher, Halimi Effendi, asked the Imperial teacher, Şemseddin Effendi, who wrote very fast, to write *Tarih-i Vassaf* with beautiful calligraphy. In addition to that, Halimi Effendi didn't take a chance and locked Molla Şemseddin in one of the rooms of his own house, saying that the Sultan gave twenty-five days to complete this task.

Molla Şemseddin pitched in with the work. According to a story, in one of those days when Molla Şemseddin was busy with writing, he realized that he was not alone in the room, but a person was sitting across from him. He started with fear but the man held his knees. He said: "Don't be afraid! We also are a human being and came to visit you."

Molla Şemseddin realized that the situation is not ordinary and that the person is from another realm. He stopped writing and asked some questions to the person: "Will Arab lands be conquered completely and joined into the protected countries of the Ottoman Empire or will they be captured by Circassians or any other groups after the return?"

He says: "Selim Khan is the officer coming to fulfill this duty. The duty of serving the Haramayn was given to him and his lineage."

"Can't it be conquered by other people? Can the conquest be easy?"

"Now, among the Rulers of Islam, God prefers the Ottoman Dynasty. Selim Khan is not out of the circle of 'the Friends of God.' He is at the level of mastership."

After telling about this experience to Hasan Can, the father of Hodja Sadeddin Effendi, the author of *Taju't-Tawarih*, Molla says: "Does the Reign of Yavuz Selim Khan take so much time?"

"He has three years."

"What is the status of Halimi Effendi who is the host of the mansion I am staying in?"

"He cannot pass beyond Damascus. He stays in Damascus."

"How about the time of my death?"

"Knowing about your own time of death is against the Divine Rules. '*Only God knows the time of the Judgement Day.... No one knows where they are going to die. Surely God is All-Knowing, All-Aware*' (Luqman 31:34)."

"Please do me a favor and warn me."

"Allah is All-Knowing. Because you are insisting this much, I am telling you that you will die on the same day with Halimi Çelebi and Selim Khan will be present at your Funeral Prayer."

He said that it is inappropriate for a person to know the end of his/her life; however, he declared that he would die on the same day with Halimi Effendi. Afterwards, he took a skullcap out of his bosom and told him to give that to Selim Khan as a gift. He took out another skullcap and said: "Give this to Halimi Çalebi." I said: "Won't you give me a souvenir," and he replied: "I did not prepare anything for you. If you do not abhor, I will give the skullcap on my head to you." I showed my desire and he gave the skullcap on his head to me. By interrupting me, he told me to write some words to see my writing. I obeyed his request. Then at that moment he disappeared from my side. I saw him walking away on the Nile. I kept watching him until he was not visible anymore. I got tired then. I was puzzled and distracted on that day."

Hodja Sadeddin Effendi took over the conversation at that moment, telling about the things he heard from his father, Hasan Can: "I saw that when Şemseddin came to visit the Caliph as usual, he sent me a message and I had to visit him. He said: 'I have news to tell you,' I met him and he told me what happened as it was explained above. He gave me the skullcap and asked me to hand it over to the Sultan. I went directly to the presence of the Sultan and told about the incident which lessons could be learned. When I delivered the skullcap as a gift he took and sniffed it. He said: 'it seems like there is something with this one. Did not he get one?' I said that I did not remember. He said: 'Go and ask him, he probably got one.' Yavuz also wanted to see the skullcap given to Molla Şemseddin. Hasan Can brought the requested one. 'He sniffed the new one longer, affected by its smell deeply and his eyes watered' by saying 'there is the smell of status,' he approved his previous words."

After Molla Şemseddin completed and brought the *Tarih-i Vassaf*, Hasan Can asked him to write the book

Hasnu Hasin by Imam Jazari. However, Molla could not start the task immediately due to the preparations for return. They arrived in Damascus. Halimi Effendi caught a severe illness. The drugs doctors him gave were useless. His sickness extended for longer periods of time and his pain was more exacerbated. Even if it was not a custom, Yavuz Sultan Selim visited his teacher.

Molla Şemseddin Effendi speaks with Hasan Can and says: "The words of that Saint about Halimi Çelebi seem to come true since doctors are incapable of doing something. However, there is nothing wrong with my health. If I did not complete *Hasnu Hasin*, my copy of *Hasnu Hasin* could be yours." These words were his last will. The next day, a note on a small paper came to Hasan Can, sent by Molla Şemseddin. It said: "I got a severe pain. I think the words of the Saint would come true. Please don't forget to give me your blessing and forgive me for any of my faults. My *Hasnu Hasin* would be yours." Molla Şemseddin showed here how important it is for a Muslim to keep his promise. When he understood that he wouldn't be able to finish the book, he promised to keep his word to give his own book. Thinking about all of this in such a great pain is also noteworthy. On the third day, the news about the death of Halimi Çelebi was heard and on the same day Molla Şemseddin died. The words of the Saint coming from the unseen realm came true. While it is not common that Sultans take part in the Funeral Prayers of the public,

Yavuz Sultan Selim personally participated in this one. He was very sad about the death of his teacher, Halimi Effendi. He was aware that the death of a master of writing like Molla Şemseddin was a big loss.

Molla Şemseddin had no heir, so his books were taken to the state treasury. The book the Sultan might be interested in was kept for him. Hasan Can took it from there and said: "Since Molla Şemseddin did not have heirs when he died, his books were transferred to the state treasury and the one worthy for the level of the Sultan was brought to the Sultan who saw *Hasnu Hasin* among the books and donated that book to me after touching its pages with his blessed fingers. I counted it as a miracle that he chose this book to give me among many others without knowing the conversations about it and he sensed my perplexity. He asked what I was surprised about and I explained everything. He suppressed his ego by saying that it is just an ordinary thing. That *Hasnu Hasin* is still with me." Although he was the person ordering Molla Şemseddin, who couldn't complete the book due to his death and bequeathed that to Hasan Can, he did not claim rights to the book. Yavuz Sultan Selim personally gave the book, which was passed to the state treasury because Molla Şemseddin didn't have a successor, to Hasan Can.

The Sultan, who knew the Persian language to an advanced degree of being able to write poems, also had a grasp of Arabic and Tatar languages. The Sultan's Divan consisting of his Persian poetry, was published centuries after him. He also had Turkish poems. He uses Selimi as his pen name for his poems.

When he told the muralist making the portrait of his grandfather that the picture didn't look like his grandfather, Ahi Çelebi, one of the men close to Bayezid II, stood next to him. Ahi Çelebi constantly complained that there were people acting with inappropriate behavior in the presence of the Sultan and said that he himself had proper manners. At that time, the painting was brought to him. After saying his opinion about the drawing, the Sultan addressed Ahi Çelebi, and said, "You as well saw the reign of the deceased" and gave the drawing to him. Without thinking, Ahi Çelebi embarrassed the artist by saying, "it is far from being perfect, he has done a sloppy job." The Sultan turned to Hasan Can and smiled. He didn't say anything. Then, by saying a Hadith about criticizing others, the Sultan mentioned that while Ahi Çelebi was acting like a person with manners, he behaves like the people he criticized with this behavior. He said: "He ranted about other people and thought that he was someone with manners but he made two mistakes in two hours."

Sultan Selim is one of the Sultans with a lot of legends about himself. Some of the legends were talked about while he was still alive. He left his son a full treasury, an excellent army and navy and great statesmen with glory. His Sultanate, even it was very short, is remembered centuries after. May God rest his soul.

MISCONCEPTIONS ABOUT
YAVUZ SULTAN SELIM

A ccording to the sources written about the history of the Ottoman Empire at the end of the 16th century, as a result of the inspections during the reign of Yavuz Sultan Selim, 40,000 people were executed completely or were sent into exile.

This information turns into a different scenario in the following years and is accepted as "40,000 Alevis were slaughtered by Yavuz Sultan Selim." It is weird that such information with unidentified sources is not discussed until today.

In this regard, the historian Feridun Emecen analyzed the resources, and made a correction about the serious charges against Yavuz Sultan Selim. It is also interesting to make accusations against Yavuz without mentioning the massacres done by Shah Ismail in Iran and Azerbaijan to propagate his religious views. The claim that "40,000 Alevis were slaughtered by Yavuz" is not included in the sources (*Selimnames*) written during

the period while the Sultan is still alive. The first reference explaining the issue of Alevi massacre with additional detailed information is the book called
Selimşahname of Idris Bitlisi.

Idris Bitlisi, who stayed very close to Sultan Selim,
and did many essential tasks and responsibilities for
him, wrote a history book of the Ottomans in Persian
called *Hasht-Bihisht* consisting of eight volumes. In this
book, he added the information related to the era of
Yavuz Sultan Selim. However, since his life was not long
enough to complete this book, his son Abulfazl Mehmed
Çelebi made corrections and a fair copy of the book.
Organizing his father's notes and adding some information reached to his era, Abulfazl completed *Selimşahname*.

In *Selimşahname*, it was indicated that the Sultan
sent an order to the administrators of the country to execute the Qizilbash group just before Chaldiran expedition while doing preparations in Edirne. He says: "Without waiting, the disciples, including three generations
back and ahead, believing Shah Ismail, deserved to be
exterminated based on the verse meaning '*without a
doubt, a person changing the faith with denial would be
strayed from the right path*;' all of them, residing in Rum
(Anatolia) towns and the nomads should be recorded."

This subject is presented as a poem in the book in
which it is written that a great number of them were executed according to this verdict. This information, which
was added to İdris Bitlisi's book by his son, was repeated

in the books of following historians such as Hodja Saded-din Effendi and Gelibolulu Mustafa Ali as if it was a fact, and the following historians caused this false information to be spread by taking this information as fact and adding even more exaggerations. Due to those who thought that everything written during the time of the Ottomans were absolutely correct, who did not have a critical approach to the sources and who did not make comparisons with the other sources of that period, and that's why this false information was narrated until today.

In the Ottoman archives, there is no information about the inspection Idris Bitlisi claimed in his book. There are no such inspection books in the Ottoman archives, not even an order for the preparation and delivery of such books to the capital. The historians living in that period did not give any information about such an incident in their books.

According to Emecen, the source of this false information could be the orders Sultan Selim sent to different regions during his fight with his brother Shahzadah Ahmed to detect the follower of him and his Qizilbash nephew, Murad. As a matter of fact, at the beginning of 1513, the names the supporters of Shahzadah Ahmed and his sons were detected and sent to the Center. Here, the names of people supporting or not supporting Shahza-dah Ahmed and the Qizilbash who went next to Shahza-dah Murad (possibly *timar* holders) from the districts of Tokat, Niksar, Gedegra, Kavak, Bafra, Sonisa, Amasya,

Çorum, Ladik, Muşali Karahisar (Akdağ Maden) were given. Other than that, no other document was found related to this issue. The number of individuals in a quite large area is only about seventy.

The reason this information was transferred with much exaggeration in the sources written later is the political and religious strife between the Ottomans and Safavids and the purpose of the historians of the 16th century emphasizing the Sunni faith to intimidate the opponents.

In some of the cadastral record books consisting of the identification of the population for the purpose of tax collection before the Battle of Chaldiran during the period of Yavuz Sultan Selim, there are some records that the Çepni villages in the plateau areas were discharged and joined Shah Ismail. There are even some official orders that if the public living in these villages returned, their resettlement would be provided with a tax exemption. If there had been an intention to massacre, their right to live would not have been recognized.

It would be helpful to remember that the punishment practiced since the era of Bayezid II for the instigators was not execution, but exile. For the survival of the state, it was obvious that there was a necessity for a severe punishment of Safavid Caliphs captured with the letters of Shah Ismail, some of the Sheiks these Caliphs contacted, and rebellious instigators. In the light of the above information, it was a huge delusion to think that it was a systematic extermination of the Qizilbash; moreover, the repetition of this mistake today is a condition that is difficult to understand.

The tomb of Sultan Selim

BIBLIOGRAPHY

Feridun Emecen, *Yavuz Sultan Selim*, İstanbul, 2010,

——, İmparatorluk Çağında Osmanlı Sultanları (II. Bayezid-Yavuz-Kanuni), İstanbul, 2011.

——, *Fetih ve Kıyamet 1453*, İstanbul, 2012.

Halil İnalcık, *Osmanlı İmparatorluğu Klasik Çağ (1300-1600)*, İstanbul, 2003.

Hoca Sadettin Efendi, *Tacü't-Tevarih*, Ed. İsmet Parmaksızoğlu, Ankara 1992.

İ.Hakkı Uzunçarşılı, *Osmanlı Tarihi*, Ankara, 1995.

İ. Hami Danişmend, İzahlı Osmanlı Tarihi *Kronolojisi*, İstanbul, 1971.

Necdet Sakaoğlu, *Bu Mülkün Sultanları*, İstanbul, 2008.

İslam Ansiklopedisi (DİA), the articles: Hadimü'l Haremeyn; Memlükler; İstanbul; Osmanlılar; Hilafet; Mekke; Medine; Selim I; and Süleyman I.

Evliya Çelebi Seyahatnamesinden Seçmeler, Ed. Nihal Atsız, İstanbul, 1990.

Faruk Sümer, *Safevi Devletinin Kuruluşunda Anadolu Türklerinin Rolü*, Ankara, 1976.

Tahsin Öz, *Hırka-i Saadet Dairesi ve Emanat-ı Mukaddese*, Ankara, 1953.

Özdemir, Hüseyin, *Osmanlı Yönetiminin Dinî Temelleri Kılıç Kalem ve İlim*, İstanbul, 2006.

Yusuf Çağlar; Salih Gülen, *Dersaadet'ten Haremeyn'e Surre-i Hümayun*, İstanbul, 2009.